7

Civilization of Paradise

Civilization
of Paradise

Revelation Poems

Asad Ali

Translated by Kabir Helminski
With Camille Helminski, Mahmoud Mostafa,
and Ibrahim Shihabi

FONS VITAE

First published in 2014 by
Fons Vitae
49 Mockingbird Valley Drive
Louisville, KY 40207
http://www.fonsvitae.com
Email: fonsvitaeky@aol.com

ISBN 978-1887752-24-4

Printed in Canada

Publication Design & Cover Art by Threshold Productions. Cover
photograph by Tim Street-Porter.

Library of Congress Cataloging-in-Publication Data

'Ali, As'ad, 1937- author.
  [Poems. Selections. English]
  Civilization of Paradise : Revelation Poems / Asad Ali ; translated
by Kabir Helminski ; with Camille Helminski, Mahmoud Mostafa,
Abed Samhuri, and Ibrahim Shihabi.
     pages cm
  ISBN 978-1-887752-24-4
  1. Arabic poetry—Syria—Translations into English. I. Helmin-
ski, Kabir Edmund, 1947- translator. II. Title.
  PJ7696.A43A2 2014
  892.7'6--dc23
                                          2013050938

Contents

The Voice of Universal Human-ness

Recently I took a walk around Point Lobos, a remarkable piece of craggy California coastline. Pounded by the curling breakers that roll in, patiently bearing the effects of millennia of weather, it is a tablet upon which nature has written its own poetry. Poetry is also seeing, seeing with more than the eyes, with the heart. At Point Lobos you read the chiseled crags, the twisted cypresses, the surging swells of turquoise, seals heads bobbing contentedly in their natural habitat.

And there at Point Lobos, at what feels like the westernmost point of the American coastline, jutting out into the sometimes fierce Pacific Ocean, I asked myself: How has the poetry of this great master of the word from Damascus altered my perception, and thus my soul?

Poetry begins in listening, and perhaps the achievement of poetry can be measured in terms of the depth and purity of that listening. Some listen to the conditioning of their society, some listen to the call of their own desires, and a very few have freed themselves from these random voices to listen to a voice that speaks with the authority of the Inmost Reality.

The human personality is fond of wearing costumes, but to forget that one is in costume is an unfortunate, if not a ludicrous condition. Literature, and especially poetry, is the search for something beyond costumes and masks. Poetry is the search for a pure language that can express that "something" that gives meaning and life to all these events and forms we witness.

Poetry is the listening that takes us home. Home is that inmost center of the human being where we are closest to the Divine Reality. Poetry is the kind of revelation that never ends. Poetry, in the case of Asad Ali, is a way of life and prayer.

His books reveal the archetypal voices of nature. In the state of consciousness from which he speaks, it is possible to listen to the eternal language of human nature. One of the effects we experience from reading or hearing these poems/psalms is a great shift in our sense of time and identity. No longer imprisoned in a succession of minutes or days, we find ourselves ascending into a timeless perspective that embraces great measures of time. No longer imprisoned in the cage of human personality, we become the companions of great beings: the Timeless Desert, the Infinitely Compassionate, the Supplicating Earth, the Universal Human.

These poems inhabit a wide universe and introduce us to new dimensions of consciousness, but they never divorce us from our own experience, nor belittle our humanness. The human adventure is given its dignity only when seen from the true perspective of this vastness.

How did we ever forget the true proportions of Being? We can only be thankful to have been reminded. Walking Point Lobos' pristine trails, inhaling the fragrances of ocean sage, being buffeted by the winds at cliff's edge, expanding into the abundant atmosphere of this sacred space and place, I thank Asad Ali and all he gives voice to.

Kabir Helminski

Asad Ali

D r. Asad Ali is an eminent Islamic thinker, spiritual visionary and a master of wisdom whose literary genius is most evident in gnosis and linguistics. He is a living spiritual master in the storied tradition of such great Sufis as Ibn Arabi and Rūmī. He received spiritual training in several Sufi schools including the Shadhiliyyah, Qadiriyyah, and Riffaiyyah schools. His writings in Arabic deal extensively with spiritual topics, with particular emphasis on Islamic Mysticism and the Sufi tradition. He is the author of many books most notably *In the Lights of the Quran*, a 25-volume multi-level poetic expression of the Quran in accordance with the seven spiritual stations of the human being. The fifth volume of *In the Lights of the Quran* has been translated into English with the title *Happiness without Death*, and was published in 1994. Dr. Ali is the founder and chairman of the World Union of Arabic Writers.

In addition he is a symbolic poet and a brilliant orator. He has written more than a thousand papers and research studies and is widely published in Arabic magazines and newspapers. Dr. Ali has a live morning broadcast on Syrian television called "The Civilization of Analogies and The Magic of Words." He also makes regular appearances on Satellite TV channels in Iraq and Lebanon.

Dr. Ali's life work is best summarized by his universal vision for our world, "We wish to establish the Civilization of Paradise here on earth."

Dr. Ali was born in 1937 in Latakia, Syria. He graduated from the School of Law at Damascus University and received his first Ph.D. in literature and theology/philosophy from Saint Joseph University in Beirut. He received his second Ph.D. in art and gnosis from Tehran University, Iran, where he studied under the eminent Rumī scholar Badiuzaman Furuzunfar. He was, until his retirement, a professor of literature, linguistic methodology and rhetoric at Damascus University. He has supervised several masters' and doctoral theses at the universities of Damascus, Beirut and Amman. He is also a member of the Syrian Research and Studies Institute. Dr. Ali currently resides in Damascus, Syria.

Camille and Kabir Helminski Consulting with Asad Ali in Damascus

On Reading These Poems

Each of these poems is related to a Surah of the Qur'an, as noted below the title of each poem. The sequence follows the order in which the Surahs were revealed, rather than the order in which they occur in the Qur'an itself. You will notice that these poems begin with the 31st Surah and continue through the 114th Surah, in temporal order, with a final six poems not associated with the Qur'an. The 1st through 30th Surah-related poems were published in another volume by us, *Happiness Without Death, Desert Hymns* (Threshold Books, 1990).

What is the relationship between the poems and the Surahs? For many years, Asad Ali would enter retreat during the holy fasting

month of Ramadan. During these months of retreat he would be in-
spired with a poem each day for thirty days. Over a period of years he
received these poems corresponding to the 114 Surahs of the Qur'an
interpreted on six successive spiritual levels of the transformed self.
As there are traditionally seven such levels of the self in Sufi teaching,
the seventh level is absent because it is considered to be transparent
and ineffable.

Nights in Damascus

*Transcriptions of Three Nights in Conversation with
Asad Ali as recorded by Mahmoud Mostafa*

Night 1

Tuesday February 22, 2005

Kabir and I are with Dr. Firas Salman who is driving us in his car up the familiar hills to the house overlooking Damascus. As the car turns slowly, I remember the shops and the narrow streets we are driving through.

I think back on how I came to be here with Kabir and how we are about to see Dr. Ali once again after so many years. It has been only three weeks since Kabir called to tell me that he was going to Syria, and asked me to join him. "I'd love to go but how can I manage this with such short notice?" I asked him. There seemed to be impossible barriers to overcome, the visa, the tickets, my work, my family visits to Chicago. My mind objected that I already had tickets booked to Chicago—what if it were hard to change the reservation? What about work, I asked myself. How can I get away from all the demands of my business on such short notice? But I ignored the nagging doubts and got on the internet to check flights. I found available flights out of Chicago at very reasonable prices. I felt more optimistic now. Maybe I could make this work after all. I had to see about the visa. Kabir said that the embassy could turn the paper work around in just a couple of days.

I called Kabir, "OK, I can make it, inshallah. I can't make the same flight out of Amsterdam that you'll be on because the connection is too short so I'll arrive in Damascus 10 hours after you do." He laughed, "That's great. I am really looking forward to this trip, especially now that I know you'll be with me." I felt elated. "We will be arriving during Ashura," I said to him. "Oh, I didn't realize this," he responded. "Yes, it will be just after the 10th of Muharram[1]. It will be a very special time."

In the car as we are driving up towards the house, Kabir and I talk about our conversation a few days before with Dr. Ali. We called to wish him happy holidays. As we talk I remembered something that Dr. Ali said to me as we were ending the call: "I will see you soon, God willing." He had said it to me with a confident and unusually low voice, as if he intended the words just for my ears. Amazing, I thought. Was this just a wish or was it an invitation? How amazing.

I think about the day's events. I arrive in Damascus in the early hours of Tuesday morning. Kabir and two other men receive me; they are Dr. Firas Salman and Bassem Issa. After we greet one other, Dr. Salman drives us into the city to our hotel named Jalaa'. In the room Kabir and I talk before going to sleep. He tells me that he has not seen Dr. Ali yet, but has talked to him on the phone. We will see him in the evening, inshallah. Kabir tells me that he had an ordeal making his flights and thought at one time that he would not be able to do it, but things worked out in the end.

He tells me that a publisher has contacted him about editing a book they had commissioned about Islam. "The book is very dry and has some strange ideas in it," Kabir tells me. "For example, the

---

1. The Tenth of Muharram is a venerated date because it commemorates the martyrdom of Imam Hussein, grandson of the Prophet Muhammad, peace be upon him, at Karbala.

author says that Islam is more focused on the afterlife than Christianity or Judaism, and that this is because it came later and is closer to the end of time!"

I shake my head, "I think that we Muslims often put the cart before the horse when it comes to our understanding and expression of Islam. We are so fixated on rules, practices, and doctrine that we don't see the real meaning of our religion. For example if we ask one hundred Muslims to tell us about Islam, ninety-nine of them will speak about The Five Pillars. But this is not a description of our Deen (our path, our Way). It's a description of important practices that people follow outwardly, but this is not the reality of our religion. It is not the message of Muhammad."

Kabir is listening intently as I continue. "A really good example of a meaningful answer to "What is Islam?" is the answer that Jafaar, the Prophet's cousin, gave to the King of Abyssinia when he asked him to tell him about this new religion that he and the small group of refugees who sought asylum in his kingdom were following. Jafaar said nothing about practices or rules, did he? Do you remember what he said?" Kabir smiles, "He said, 'We were lost in ignorance, we abused each other . . ..'" He pauses, trying to remember, so I continue, "the strong among us devoured the weak, we severed the bonds of mercy between us, and we abused our women until there came from among us a prophet whom we loved and trusted, and he changed us, he taught us to be merciful, to be truthful, to be just, to protect the weak and helpless. So we followed him and believed in him."

I pause to gather my thoughts. "Jafaar's answer was clear. Islam is that which transforms our hearts, that turns us from animals motivated by fear and pleasure to humans capable of love and sacrifice. Islam is what brings us out of the darkness into the light. This is the Deen of Muhammad. And its practice depends on trust and love between human beings. No one would have become Muslim if he or she did not love the Prophet, if they did not trust him. Can you imagine what would have happened if the Prophet's message was all

15

about rules and dogma? The practices came later to build and reinforce character. In fact it is recorded in the Seerah[2] that the Prophet taught his companions faith first, then he taught them practices. There is so much, so much that we have lost in our understanding of this religion. It's very sad." I look down wondering if I said too much.

"Maybe you should be writing a book," Kabir says, smiling.

"Can you imagine what would have happened if the Prophet had lambasted people with rules and doctrine and legalisms? Who would have followed him except the Bin Ladens and Taliban of his time?" I ask rhetorically. To myself I say that there would have been no Ali or Abu Bakr. There would have been none of the great souls throughout the ages who were the fruit of that blessed tree of Muhammad's message.

"I'll ask you to help me with the rewriting of this book," Kabir says, interrupting my thoughts.

"I would love to help with it in any way I can, inshallah."

The car makes a right turn past a brightly lit falafel shop. This is the street; we're very close now.

"Welcome to Syria, Abu Eid! I am so happy you are here. Today is my last day of seclusion," Dr. Ali told me when I called earlier in the day to see when he would receive us. "I will be out in the evening after the night prayer. What did you do today in the morning?"

"We had breakfast and then we visited John the Baptist," I replied.

"Good. Now you should visit Lady Zeynab, Lady Ruqayyah, and Sheikh Ibn Arabi. Then you can come and visit me," he said with his usual effervescence.

Kabir and I understand that this is not just a casual suggestion, and so we duly gather ourselves and head out of the hotel. In a few minutes we are on our way to the Great Lady's tomb. We arrive at the gateway to the mosque of Lady Zeynab, the granddaughter of the Prophet and one of the most holy and revered people for Muslims

---

2. Accounts of the Prophet's life.

who know her as the Mother of the Helpless or just as The Lady. We enter the sanctuary of her tomb, which is filled with visitors, and we offer our prayers. The walls of the mosque are covered in a motif of glass mirrors giving it an aura of shimmering lights.

As I prostrate my head to the ground I hear a voice. It's a woman's voice, sweet and tender and yet firm and towering at the same time, "I have never seen a day like this day," she says. I weep with sorrow at her words, wondering what the 13th of Muharram was like for Lady Zeynab. Was this the day that she arrived in Damascus from Kerbala[3] along with the rest of the survivors of Imam Hussein's family? Was this the day that the tyrant Yazeed mocked her, when she answered him in her noble way with the Quran, "God is the Sovereign Owner of the Dominion . . .."? Was this the day they buried the severed head of her martyred brother and the rest of her brothers and cousins who stood with him to the end at Kerbala? What was this day for her? I finish my prayer and sit silently in remembrance next to Kabir for a while.

As we walk out into the courtyard of the mosque we see a group of people gathered in a circle with a man reciting an ode in Farsi to Imam Hussein. Some people are weeping as they listen to the words. Outside the gate we see a group of people marching with large black and gold banners in commemoration of Imam Hussein. They are chanting and striking their chests with their fists. They come to a stop in front of the gate of Lady Zeynab and there they continue their chanting. The atmosphere is charged with emotion and determination. It is as if the tragedy of Kerbala had just happened recently. It is remarkable how the memory of this seminal event in the history of the Muslim community has been kept alive in the hearts of the lovers of the Prophet and his family for so many centuries.

We take a taxi to the sanctuary of Lady Ruqayyah, the young daughter of Imam Hussein who died of her sorrow over the killing of her father. Her sanctuary is also full but quieter than Lady Zeynab's. We offer our prayers and spend time in silence before her tomb. As

---

3. The place of Imam Hussein's martyrdom.

we walk around the neighborhood of the mosque trying to find our bearing, we stop at a sweets shop and pick up an assortment of pastries as a gift for our evening meeting with Dr. Ali.

From Lady Ruqayyah we take another taxi to the hills above Damascus where Ibn Arabi is buried. We enter the familiar place and offer our prayers. As I sit silently, the jet lag catches up to me and I begin to doze off. I can hear the faint voice of a woman praying behind the green curtain opposite me. Then I see a line dividing two spaces and a voice tells me that this is the Barzakh, the threshold between two worlds.

As we leave Sheikh Ibn Arabi's sanctuary we are surrounded by poor people begging. They are mostly women but there are two or three old men as well. Kabir asks me if I have any Syrian pounds and I nod and go to one of the vendors to make change so I can distribute the money among the people. The vendor, who seems to know the poor folk surrounding me, tells me who is in most need of help. Each gets a share of the charity, and says prayers for us. I feel blessed that we are able to give something to those in need at this blessed place. We get into our waiting taxi and return to the hotel where we rest before Dr. Firas comes to take us to Dr. Ali's home.

The car turns left and creeps up the steep driveway to the house. We walk past a black Mercedes sedan parked in front of the green iron gate through which we enter into the garden of the house. I remember our last farewells seven years ago in this same garden before this very gate. I remember how we embraced and how Dr. Ali prayed for us and gave us as a parting gift, a prayer for us to invoke whenever we were in need, "Help me in my need, O You whose eye never sleeps!" We walk through the seasonally barren flower canopy and enter through the back door of the house.

"Welcome, welcome! Peace upon you," Dr. Ali says as he kisses Kabir and then me. His face is as bright as I remembered it. His voice is full with the vigor of life. He smiles broadly when he sees us and he is filled with delight as he introduces us. The living room is filled with people. I recognize the faces of our dear friends and devoted students of Dr. Ali. There is Dr. Ali Himdan, the talented calligraphic artist, and there is Ramadan, Dr. Ali's nephew. I look around and see the room is just as it was seven years ago. The windows are covered with green drapes, and the walls are adorned with Quranic verses and pictures of the sanctuaries of the Prophet and his family. The room is filled with books neatly arranged on shelves with the title of volumes colorfully written across the books' bindings. The furniture is the same—simple chairs and couches with Damascene patterned cushions. We have entered into the presence of our master, our living Mawlana.

Dr. Ali begins by introducing one of his visitors, Dr. Ahmad Imran, who is the retired head of the Syrian Lawyers Union and Dean of the School of Law at the University of Damascus. As he introduces him he affectionately holds his hand in his. "Now he is the head of the Retirees Union!" Dr. Ali says jokingly. He points to the bookshelves, "Here is Dr. Imran's encyclopedia right next to your books, Kabir." He then proceeds to explain to Dr. Imran about Kabir and Camille and their work and publications. "One of his books that I particularly love is *The Knowing Heart*," he tells Dr. Imran with pride. "The reason I love it is that the bond between us has always been that of the heart."

He goes on to explain, "When you read the word H-E-A-R-T from East to West it means 'You see Him' in Arabic but if you read it from West to East and dive into its meanings you will see that He is Art. God is Art." He then points to the two book collections on the shelf beneath the large volume of *In the Shades of the Quran*. "So the two of you are neighbors under the shades of the Quran, a Western doctor and an Eastern doctor. And here you meet. You have arrived before me because this is the first day for me out of seclusion. This is the first day that I come out in Muharram. I couldn't see you sooner because I looked scary in my beard, just like a terrorist! A little bit like Kabir," he jokes pointing at Kabir's beard, "So I just shaved today and came out and you are the first people that I have received this month. I even stretched it a bit because I was supposed to stay in seclusion all of today too and come out tomorrow. But by your intercession I was able to come out sooner."

Dr. Imran apologizes and says that if he knew this, he wouldn't have come today, "No, on the contrary, I know now your dearness to Hussein and his people, that he lets you intercede on my behalf to get me out of prison," he says and breaks out laughing with delight. "And this is Mahmoud Mostafa, Abu Eid, who is our translator and a very good friend of Sheikh Ibn Arabi. And of course anyone who is a good friend of Ibn Arabi—between me and him is a relationship that is beyond words. We have between us words without words. He is living in America and is of Egyptian origin."

He then goes around and introduces the others in the room. There is our new friend Bassem Issa from Holland, and also Dr. Imran Imran, son of Dr. Ahmad and the head of the lawyers union in Tarsus. "I tell him one Imran made Moses and Mary and you are two Imrans together—so what will you do?" He jokes and breaks out in his boyish laughter. Then he moves to an engineer, Salman Subeih, who speaks German, Russian and other European languages. Then there is the young poet, Azdeshir Khalil. Then on to Dr. Ali Himdan, the artist who draws calligraphic figures of great beauty. Then to two young men who are taping the gathering, Kinan Hussein and Sam Yusuf.

He then turns back to Kabir and asks about the family: "Tell us, how are Camille, Shams, Matthew and the Queen Carolina?" He affectionately pronounces their daughter Cara's name as *Caroleena*. He laughs and then tells Dr. Imran how Cara was just a little girl when she first came to Damascus and how she left her teeth here and they planted them in the garden. Now several large trees have grown out of that spot and they are called "Caroleena's Teeth." He goes on to tell a story about a girl named Carolina whose mother was semidivine. This Carolina died but as they were burying her, her mother held her hands. The girl would not let go of her mother's hand and was thus brought back to life.

More visitors stream into the living room as we are talking.

Dr. Ali introduces Dr. Ma`an Ali. One of the young ladies brings a bunch of yellow narcissus flowers as a gift. "What does narcissus mean to you?" Dr. Ali asks Kabir. "Purity," he replied after a long reflective pause. "Does it mean something historical?" Dr. Ali asks him further. "Yes, it was another name for one of the people of the Prophet's family," Kabir says.

"No, no. It was the name of a young man who was searching for himself. He wanted to know who he was. It is an old legend. He saw his face reflected in a pool of water and thought he had found himself so he kept on looking at his own face and this flower sprouted at that spot and was given his name. That is in the past. In the future Narcissus is a name of a woman who is a descendant of St. Peter. She is the mother of Muhammad Ibn Al Hassan Al Askari who is the awaited Mahdi and the Owner of Time, who will arrive and fill the world with justice and equity."

Kabir then gives Dr. Ali copies of his latest books published with Camille. Kabir explains the Education Project they are engaged with, and speaks of its goals. As we are talking, Dr. Imran is carrying on a side conversation with Dr. Ali, wanting to know about Kabir. Dr. Ali somehow manages to listen to him and also maintain his attention with us. He lets Dr. Imran know that Kabir is doing very important work for humanity and that his work is known throughout the world. People around the room want to know where Kabir is from. "Polish ancestry," are the whispers in the background.

Dr. Imran is visibly disinterested in the conversation and wants to engage Dr. Ali in his own conversation, but Dr. Ali keeps him under control. Kabir goes on to explain how people in America are thirsty to know more about Islam and that our work is to present Islam in an undistorted way to them. Dr. Ali explains to Dr. Imran that we are working within the American environment to present an Islam that is less distorted by cultural biases.

Dr. Imran listens for a while and then gets up to leave, but Dr. Ali stops him, "Before you go I want to explain about RETIRING." He then goes on to explain to us that Dr. Imran was the foremost lawyer in Syria, but that at that time was not involved in the Sufi path. After he retired from his profession he started working with Dr. Ali and wrote nineteen books under his guidance. "The word Retirement in Arabic is Taqa`ud, which literally means to sit down. So retired people are called Mutaqa`id, which means someone who has sat down or has nothing to do, and in our Syrian slang we pronounce it Mut Qa`idan which means to die sitting down.

In writing his book about Imam Ali, Dr. Ali continues, he found three of Imam Ali's words which opened up new horizons and galaxies of meaning.

"Imam Ali says, 'At Tuqa Ra'isul Akhlaq,' meaning that Tuqa is the head of good character. Tuqa means purity of faith, and the clarification of principles. It means to truly stand for the oneness of the Unique One (Tawheed ul Ahad). This word (same as Taqwa) comes from the root WQA which is protection; we say an ounce of protection is better than a pound of cure. So Tuqa means the protection of the Nafs from any kind of associations with God so the servant knows the Unique One. Now Taqa`ud is made up of two words Tuqa and `Ud which means come back, come back Abu Eid, return!" he says to me laughingly. "The Nafs returns to truth and sees its Originator, light upon light. So when this master of ours," Dr. Ali says pointing to Dr. Imran, "came back to Taqwa he wrote nineteen books in the span of ten years nineteen books—important books about secularism, feminism, philosophy, the common ground between Christianity and Islam and so on. It's one of the ways of our dance school! He dances very well! This is why we gave him the title of "the head of the retirees" since it means the returning to purity, to clarity." Dr. Imran is visibly pleased with the accolades Dr. Ali has given him.

Dr. Ali continues, "From a psychological point of view when one is employed, one is bound by the limitations of one's job. But when you leave your job you are in absolute freedom, you sleep whenever you want, get up whenever you want, work whenever you want. So we believe that the youthfulness of purity comes when preoccupations are left behind."

Dr. Imran finds an opening to speak, "For forty-three years I spent my life with criminals of all kinds. By God, I did not live my true life until I started writing. The people I associated with before always took from my mind and gave back nothing, but writing gave back to me."

Dr. Ali responds, "When I attended the lecture of Dr. Nawaf Shibli, he told me that before I arrived he felt that his capacity was being bled. Everything around him was sucking his energy out of him. When I started speaking he started to feel he was being filled. The idea here is that the interaction of free minds is like the connection of wires that bring light. Loose individual wires don't light anything up. Maybe you can use them to tie things together, but they cannot light up anything. Imam Ali says that God gave you the keys of His treasury when he gave you permission to call to Him. He said, 'Call upon Me and I will respond to you.' So when He said to you 'call upon Me,' He guaranteed to you that He would respond. This is from the verse, *'If My servants ask you about Me, I am near. I respond to those who call to me. So let them respond to Me and let them have faith in Me so that perhaps they will be guided.'* Kabir needs no translation of this part!" He interrupts me, laughing, "This is the Quran and he knows it. We just remind him of it and he knows it."

"I think that every time you are able to clear your mind of pre-occupations you return to being a child. This is why Jesus said, 'You will not enter The Dominion until you return and become like children,' that is until you have no preoccupations but God. This is the idea of continuous childhood, this is the idea of the returning to purity, of Tuqa`ud. When Pharaoh brought the sorcerers, Moses brought his staff and it devoured all of their magic. After this the sorcerers believed in Moses. So the stick convinced them. It didn't force them, it convinced them."

Dr. Imran now talks about his ideas concerning the staff of Moses, "The staff is Satan. It is what tempted Eve, it is what devoured the sorcerers' staffs, and it is what brought the plagues upon Pharaoh's land. So what is this staff?" he asks Dr. Ali.

Dr. Ali listens intently and then with a broad smile he asks Dr. Imran's son, "What is this behind you on the wall, Imran?" To which the son answers, "It is God's Most Beautiful Names."

"How many are they?" Dr. Ali asks.

"They are ninety nine." Imran answers.

"Ninety nine, this is symbolic. There is a book of prayers called Al Jawshan Al Kabir, The Great Shield, which has 1,000 of the Most Beautiful Names. Among these names there is The Life Giver and the Slayer. The staff has in it that which saves and that which destroys."

Dr. Imran continues on with his train of thought seemingly unaffected by what Dr. Ali is saying, "The one name that belongs only to God is Allah. If you take away the article Al, you can name anyone by these names, but if you include the article Al, then it only belongs to God and no one can be named by that name."

Dr. Ali is listening with amusement and bursts out, "Unless he is Iranian! I have an author friend whose name is Allah Azar Wardi! He named himself Allah just like that! You are right of course," he assures his friend and then turning to us he explains, "Dr. Ahmed is pointing out that the name of the essence is unique and is specific to Allah's essence, but from it branch countless names and for each name there are countless attributes."

Dr. Imran continues with his train of thought. "Allah comes from Aliha which means to be perplexed. That is, God is the one whom minds are at a loss to comprehend and are in perplexity over Him. If you remove the first Aliph then what remains is Lillah: To God is all that is in heaven and earth. If you remove the Lam then what remains is Lahu: To God is the command and the prohibition. If you remove the second Lam then what remains is Hu: and you come back to the origin!"

"We come back to the infinite Hu," Dr. Ali affirms.

"He is unseen, unknowable. Many people talk about the Beautiful Names, but those names are for calling unto God. When you are burdened by something, you call upon God with the particular name that can relieve your burden," Dr. Imran continues to explain.

"Yes, you turn to Him whatever your need may be," Dr. Ali agrees as he sips his tea.

"But the name of the divine essence is only for Him." Dr. Imran says.

"Yes," replies Dr. Ali, "but the gnostics say that the divine essence is an infinite ocean of pure, sweet water. Khidr has a very beautiful saying recorded in a book called *The Drinking Sources of the Spirits*. He says that between the servant and the Creative One are thousands of thousands of drinking sources even though He is closer to us than our jugular veins. These drinking sources are the different paths; each path is a place where we drink, where we find what we need. Each place is one of the Beautiful Names. When you need healing you call out Ya Shafi, O Healer! When you need sustenance you call out Ya Razzaq, O Sustainer! When you need ability you call out Ya Qadir, O Able One! But that drinking place in practice takes you to the ocean itself, because all sources of guidance, whether in the form of a prophet or a book or a saint, are coming from one source. When you contemplate the word Hadiy, or guidance, and follow it back to its source, you will find that it is Yadih, or His Hand. His Power is over everything, His Power is over every Beautiful Name, and His essence is in every name. This is why for the Unifiers, all the names and attributes are but one. They don't even ask God for anything; they just say, 'Your knowledge of my state makes my asking of You unnecessary!'"

Dr. Imran is nodding in agreement throughout and then when he finds an opening he cracks a joke and Dr. Ali high-fives him and expresses his pleasure at it. Someone else says that there are as many ways to God as there are breaths in creation. "Yes, Imam Ali said this," Dr. Ali affirms.

Dr. Imran then speaks. "Someone told me he doesn't believe that God exists. So I told him, let's suppose I show you a book and then I tell you that the letters were just wandering around randomly and then they formed words that have meaning on their own and then the words formed sentences that have meanings on their own, then paragraphs with meanings on their own and then a book with meaning on its own—and then they somehow made their way to a printing press and got printed on their own and then distributed on their own. What would you say about me? Wouldn't you say I am crazy? Well every being in existence is more complicated than a book. Even the wing of a butterfly is more complex."

Dr. Ali nods in agreement and adds, "Jesus said, referring to the jasmine tree, that not even Solomon with his dominion can make the like of the jasmine flowers."

"What he is trying to say is that there is nothing in existence that is not for Him. We are for God and unto Him we shall return," Dr. Imran says, quoting the Quran.

"And it is our good fortune that we are for God." Dr. Ali says with a warm smile as he looks around the room.

Dr. Imran goes on with his discourse, "Everything the body needs is from the earth. And all that the spirit needs is from the Creator of the earth." He proclaims and points his index finger upwards. Dr. Ali puckers his lips and says, "Hmm, in a way . . ." Dr. Imran continues on, "Not everything the mind needs is from the earth, but all material needs are from the earth. So we are from the earth and we return to the earth. Dust returns to dust, but the other part returns to its Originator."

"We have a name for Imam Ali, which is Father of the Dust. So the dust is the brother of Hussein and Hasan," Dr. Ali says as he smiles broadly with a flash of anticipation in his eyes, "Hasan and Hussein have spirit."

But Dr. Imran interrupts him before he can finish, "Father of the Dust is a description," he objects.

"Just a second, permit me to take you to the meaning," Dr. Ali says to him smiling, "Turab, or dust, is Tura Abb which means to see the father, which means that there is nothing in existence without spirit. This is our way of seeing things. We see the entire universe as

the Living One. This whole universe is the Living One, Al Hayy."
He repeats the name for emphasis. Those in the room who are clos-
est to Dr. Ali are smiling as they listen to his words, while Dr. Imran
seems absorbed in his thoughts with his head bowed down and his
fingers turning his prayer beads. "The dust, the air, the rocks, and
the trees are all The Living One. Al Qayyum, the Eternally Subsist-
ing One, refers to the structure of your own existence. What do you
take from Life? How much do you take from the Living One? That
is your subsistence and also your resurrection. You may come from
America, or from Tarsus, or from Holland, or from Armenia, so that
is the share of the Living One that subsists in you to the extent of
your intention and ambition—because the giving is in proportion to
the intention. In reality my theory is very powerful; it is that at any
age, at any time, in any state, when you empty of everything but
Him, then He will aid you towards purity and strength and ability.
This is it. The source of the theory of unity, Tawheed, is to return to
purity, to protect one's heart, to surrender oneself to God."

Dr. Ali is speaking with his entire being, his hands are gesturing
emphatically. His head and upper body are turned to face Dr. Imran
squarely, and he leans forward as he stresses the point about unity
and surrender. "Now, how does someone walk on water? How long
does it take for a tree to grow? But Jesus with one word brought
Lazarus back to life," he says. He grips the arms of the chair with
both hands as if he is about to spring up from it, and then he pauses.

Dr. Imran finds another opening and says, "What about the
Samiri who took a handful of dust from beneath the feet of Moses
and from it fashioned the idol of the golden calf? Just a handful
of dust had enough energy in it for him to do this." Dr. Ali laughs
in agreement with him. "Yes, this is even greater than Jesus raising
the dead. The Samiri is able to create a great idol and influence the
people of Israel with just a handful of dust from the feet of Moses!"

Dr. Ali then leans forward in his chair and places his hand on his
brow in a thinking posture. Leaning forward towards us he says, in
his playful manner, "Now with Tassawuf . . . you know I forgot Tas-

sawuf during Ashura! But now I am starting to remember a little bit! It's knocking on the gates of my mind now. Isn't there something in Tassawuf known as following in the footsteps—Qadamiyya? An example of this is when you walk on the snow, and when I come I place my foot in exactly the same spot as your footprint so I won't sink in the snow. Now with Moses, I would like to make a staff like his, so I get a stick to lean on. But then how can I make it turn into a great serpent that devours all the others? How can I do this," he asks looking at Dr. Imran who answers, "I'll tell you how," but Dr. Ali continues to ask with a low voice as he points down at his foot with his index finger, "How? Following in the footsteps?" Dr. Imran proceeds with his answer, "Prophet Muhammad made it clear that it is through calling down the wrath of God on whoever did wrong . . . .."

Dr. Ali shakes his head, "No, this is a different matter altogether. We are not talking about arguing; we are talking about peaceful action. I am asking how I can make a staff like Moses," he says, leaning forward towards us and smiling with anticipation. Dr. Imran leans back in his chair and looks down at his prayer beads, frowning as he rolls them one by one through his fingers. "Or how do I make a word like Jesus' word? Or . . . you visited John the Baptist today didn't you?" he asks us, "How do I make a river in which I can baptize people?"

Dr. Imran interjects yet again, "You can't, because Peter, when he went to the water, couldn't walk on it and Jesus told him, 'If you had faith, you would have been safe.'" He says this with a laugh, but Dr. Ali raises a finger to stop him and says, "No, I can do it if I follow the footsteps of Jesus, if I follow the footsteps of Jesus and do not associate anything with God. If I follow the footsteps of Jesus, and do not have doubts, if I walk in the footsteps of John and have no doubts."

He then teasingly turns to Dr. Imran and asks him, "You are friends with Muntajab aren't you?" at which Dr. Imran chuckles and nods, "Yes I like him very much!" Dr. Ali playfully says, "Really? You're really friends? Listen to what he says then." He goes on to explain how this great Sufi poet told of divine love. "The divine wine, the ferment of being, of spirit, was like a lake in the beginning before God commanded existence into becoming and into differentiation. So Muntajab says he drank from this wine until he got drunk and he kept on singing, singing, singing until the great name, the one that puts the world into motion became manifest to him and he cried out, 'Mawlana, Master, O My Master, a Master who, if I say I am His obedient servant, the entire universe to its farthest reaches would obey me.' So when he proclaimed God as his Master everything came under his command. This is also in the Sacred Traditions where God says, 'Obey Me, My servant and you will become like Me.' So following in the footsteps is becoming the like of. Through obedience you will reach everything. *Through obedience, through purity of obedience, through purity of obedience, through purity of faith,*" he says, shaking a finger at us for emphasis. Dr. Imran puts in a few words of his own, "Jesus said several times in the Bible, 'If you walk the straight path you will become the children of your Father who is in Heaven.'"

Dr. Ali asks, "But how can you become like this?"

Dr. Imran interrupts him, "Anyone when he begins to pray says, 'Our Father who art in Heaven,' but He is not his father, it's symbolic." Dr. Ali interjects, "My Father and your Father, Jesus said."

Dr. Imran continues, "I found that the words Father and Lord. Lord, Rabb, really mean Educator in ancient Aramaic. A Gentile woman called out to Jesus saying, 'Rabbunee, or my educator, my daughter is seriously ill,' but he did not pay attention to her. His disciples told him to answer her because she was raising her voice and crying out to him for help. He said, 'I only came to the lost sheep of Israel.' So she prostrated herself before him and said, 'But my daughter is very ill.' He said, 'It is not good that the bread of the children be thrown to the dogs.' She said, 'But the dogs eat from the crumbs of the table of their masters, my master.' He said, 'Your faith has benefited you, woman, and because of it your daughter is cured.'"

Dr. Ali is listening very intently and with emotion to these words. His eyes are closed and he appears to be crying as he listens. Now he heaves a sigh and is visibly moved as he listens to Dr. Imran recounting the story of the Gentile woman in the Bible. He continues to sit with his eyes closed and his thumb and index finger pressed against his lips in deep contemplation as he absorbs the meanings of this story. He seems to be in conversation within himself as he listens.

Dr. Imran continues, "Jesus then asked her to give him water, but she replied that he was a Jew and she was not and that he shouldn't even be talking to her. He told her, 'if you knew who is asking you, you would have asked me to drink because I am that water from which if you drink you would never feel thirst.' She told him, 'maybe you wish to be like our father, Jacob who dug this well for us. From where can I draw water for you?' He told her 'Send for your husband.' She said, 'I have no husband.' He said, 'You have five husbands and the one who is with you now is not your husband.' She said, 'They tell us to prostrate on this mountain and you tell us to prostrate in the temple.' He said, 'Woman, there will come a day when you will not know where to prostrate and upon what to prostrate, but we know how and where to prostrate and salvation will only be from the Jews."

Dr. Ali continues to listen intently with his eyes shut and moves his lips as if he is speaking with someone, then he finally straightens himself and speaks, "The subject, as Christ saw it, when at that time he said 'Rabbunee,' means My Beloved, My Beloved Rabb. When he cried out 'Rabbunee' he was straightening the warped understanding of the disciples who believed that he was exclusively for them, that they were the chosen ones. This is that original chauvinism that they possessed. So when he called out Rabbunee, he caused the woman to speak and she spoke like him. He who is the humble Messiah was out-humbled by the woman's humility. He communicated to her on the spiritual level and directed her to speak in this way to him. So when he told her that dogs should not eat the food of children, he was reflecting his disciples' way of thinking. And when she responded by telling him that dogs eat the crumbs that fall from their masters' table, what was meant by this dialogue is that this kind of wrong thinking is not suitable for his followers, they should think humbly, lovingly because God is the Rabb of dogs, of flies, and of everything."

Dr. Imran starts to speak, but this time Dr. Ali gives him no opening and continues driving his message, "No, no, Rabbunee especially. We are now talking about this particular aspect of the Most Beautiful Names. Rabbunee is this Rabb who leaves no ant, no hoopoe, not a single atom of anything without His nourishing care penetrating it completely, thereby educating all. In this way the gentile woman becomes the one who educates Christ, meaning that she comes to his aid so he can teach his disciples. This is exactly the same way that the ant and the hoopoe taught Solomon. The hoopoe came to Solomon and Solomon wanted to kill it, but the hoopoe told him, 'I know something that you don't,' and he informed Solomon about Bilqis, the Queen of Sheba—and things happened after that. So the bird that Solomon wanted to kill became his teacher."

Dr. Imran steers the conversation in a different direction by talking about Martin Luther and his writings about Judaism and how he finds that Luther's position on Judaism in relation to Christianity changed from total support to total rejection. Dr. Ali listens to him and then says, "I have three observations. The first is that Dr. Imran can be a narrator of the story of Hussein because he is able to tell a story and bring someone like me to tears. The second is that the Patriarch Hazeen of Syria has commented on the words of Dr. Imran and said that we need to reflect on Dr. Imran's writings about Islam and Christianity and their relationship to one another. The Patriarch says that Dr. Imran's writings are deep in their literary, legalistic, and religious meanings. The third point is that a poor servant like me reads his writings in a new way.

"With the staff I am shown some new aspects. For example concerning Luther—who is Luther compared to Bill Gates, who says 'I am going to change the world?' I saw a picture of Bill Gates' standing with his arms folded across his chest, proclaiming that he would change the world through Microsoft. He wants to make a cell phone that will let Imran call any continent from an airplane; he wants to make a phone that will let a mother call her daughter who is on a different continent. Now our minds have a renewed understanding of the Quran, an understanding in a new light. New gadgets are not new knowledge for us because we have the knowledge of Solomon in the Noble Quran. 'The one who had some knowledge from the book said, I will bring it to you before you blink. So when he saw it secured next to him he said, 'This is from the favor of my Rabb to test me whether I will be thankful or whether I will deny. Whoever is thankful is thankful for himself and whoever denies, indeed my Rabb is noble, generous, and free of any want.' Who is saying these words? It is Solomon, the Wise, Solomon the Wise by his nature."

Here Dr. Ali laughs with delight at his own words and claps his hands together as if to announce something new. "Solomon by his nature is a Jewish prophet, but when we follow his story in the same Surah and see his actions with the Queen of Sheba, we find that this Jewish prophet is a caller to Islam among the Arabs! You have to read the story holistically. When the Queen receives his message it says, 'Come to me as Muslims.' And in the end Bilqis (Sheba) says, I have submitted along with Solomon to the Rabb of the worlds. So if I want to read the Quran in the purest way without any accretions or interference, I find that the assumptions of all the researchers of the East and West when it comes to the idea of religion are off the mark.

"If we take the letters that make up the Quran, we find that the 28 letters that we arrange and rearrange become an endless, unfathomable number of letters," he says. Then pointing to Kabir, Dr. Ali challenges him. "You think you know English? You think you speak English? Count for me the English letters, let me see your big philosopher with your hundred books and I don't know what. Come on count them for me. Do you know the alphabet by heart?" he asks, leaning forward towards Kabir with his hand resting on Dr. Imran's knee as he breaks out laughing again and clapping. "Come on, recite them!" Kabir smiles and begins to recite, "A B C D . . ." then breaks out laughing, and so does everyone else. "You see, in the Arabic Alphabet we have ABJD HWZ HTI KLMN . . ." Dr. Ali explains, "And in English we have K-L-M-N. What I mean to show is that there is a single alphabet—the alphabet of all humanity. It's my conviction that this is clear evidence that all the languages on earth are united in their alphabet. Imam Ali wastes no time with letters. He says, 'Knowledge is a single point!'"

Here Dr. Imran sits up and leans forward to speak, "I'll tell you a story . . ." but Dr. Ali keeps on going, "All of knowledge is a single point." Dr. Imran leans back in his chair and listens, "I want to solve a problem that is in this world," Dr. Ali says gesturing with his hand for us to pay attention, "This is a real problem. People are slaughtering each other over their identities. This is because they are in the ignorance that Imam Ali alluded to when he said, 'Knowledge is a single point.' Just as all letters are united in a point, so is humanity all united in a single parent, Adam."

Finding an opening, Dr. Imran once again interjects his thoughts. "Modern science has shown us that all living things are composed of the same basic protein structures." Dr. Ali listens to him with an amused smile. "This is correct. But depending on the combinations of these structures you sometimes get a bee whose structure yields nourishment and healing, while at other times you get a fly whose structure yields microbes and disease. Therefore we want to know how to choose between structures and to bring them together into a bee-like togetherness, like the bee that brings goodness."

Dr. Ali then looks across the room to Imran the son and referring to Dr. Imran says, "You'll see tomorrow, he's becoming the king of the discussion. I have only been sparring with him to prepare him for tomorrow's meeting. We know now that he is able to spar with Solomon, Luther, and so and so. He's a champion, a champion! May God strengthen you and help you, inshallah. Every sitting with you brings forth a book! I am so happy, so happy that you are here. And I am prepared to attend, if you are prepared to translate everything,

Abu Eid. We will attend tomorrow's meeting," he says, as Dr. Imran and his son get up and take their leave of the gathering.

We sit down and I take the opportunity to present Dr. Ali with a gift that I brought for him. It's a Chinese calligraphy of The Most Beautiful Names done by a Chinese Muslim living in America. Dr. Ali unwinds the scroll to show it to the people in the room. "This is very nice. There is nothing better than that a servant gives his Creator as a gift to another servant."

"Let us return now to our particular concerns," he says, addressing Kabir, "because we have the understanding." However, when I translate this to Kabir he asks me, "Is this the meaning of Al Fahm in English? Understanding? There is no other meaning?" I look around the room for help and everyone breaks out laughing. One of the ladies says, "Alf Hamm." Dr. Ali repeats, "Yes, Elisa says Alf Hamm." And one of the men translates, "One thousand concerns." Dr. Ali leans over and explains, "Al Fahm, understanding, in Arabic is also Alf Hamm, a thousand concerns, and every Hamm, concern, requires a thousand Himmas[4]. When this is so then we can read the Ta Seen of understanding among the Tawaseen of Hallaj for example," he says and breaks out laughing in delight at the interplay of words and meanings. I find myself at a loss to translate what he has just said. Just then another guest arrives and the conversation is interrupted as Dr. Ali introduces Mr. Muneer Al Shwaiki to Kabir and introduces Kabir to him. "This is Kabir, the one you hear about in our talks, the one who wrote *The Knowing Heart*." He asks Kabir how his heart guided him to write this book. "Tell the story of the heart as it writes about the knowing heart!" he says laughing.

"When I journeyed from the mind, when I left the mind, I began to see from the heart. I saw the need to go beyond the intellect. I began to see through the heart with the encouragement of Mawlana," Kabir responded with a smile, "and to understand that the heart is the most important instrument of knowledge that helps us understand the relationship between the finite and the infinite."

---

4. Earnest intentions.

Dr. Ali holds Kabir's arm and says, "This is the same issue that Rumī faced. Jalālu'ddin Rumī was a philosopher who used to speak from logic until the dervish Shamsuddin came to him and communicated something to him from his heart. Rumī asked him to teach him something of this radiance that he saw in him, but Shamsuddin told him, 'This has nothing to do with you. Stick to your philosophy!' And this drove Jalālu'ddin mad, mad. He started whirling and he continues to whirl for a hundred thousand years because Shamsuddin melted all thought away from him. Shamsuddin directed the rays of the Sun upon him until it melted away all of his preoccupations and struck the heart of the matter. When he collided with the Ocean he was drowned and when Jalālu'ddin drowned he became Mawlana. He became the seafarer who has to keep whirling lest he drown. He has to keep turning in order to stay in balance for him not to drown in the fire of radiance."

"OK, now I want to ask a question that I asked before. I just want to test your memory. Which Surah inspired Jalālu'ddin to produce the Mathnawī?" Kabir immediately answers, "Al Qasas." At this Dr. Ali claps his hands and laughs, "Yes, bravo! Great!" Kabir looks at him lovingly and says, "How can I forget?" Dr. Ali responds, "Last time you didn't know the answer to this question, and the answer came from an Iranian youth, the son of Qazwini. Anyway, now tell me about your new projects."

One of the guests, Ma`an Ali, wishes to invite us to a late dinner, "Thank you, Dr. Ali is our dinner, the food of our hearts," Kabir replies, politely declining the invitation. Dr. Ali laughs, "He only likes to eat me! Eat my flesh and drink my blood!" he says, repeating the words of Christ. "These are very profound words of Jesus. It's a wonder of wonders." He tells us, "I am writing a book called *The Meeting of Hussein and The Messiah*. They have met upon 'the reconciling principle,'" he tells us, using a phrase from the Quran, "This is a new understanding of the reconciling principle, not the current understanding. The reconciling principle is sacrifice. It means to truly present yourself as a sacrifice the way Jesus did and the way

Hussein did. This is why their meeting is in the reconciling principle —which is to present one's essence for the sake of others."

"We had a guest, Mr. Brian Cox from California. He is part of a group called the Abrahamic Society. We asked him, 'Are you really Abrahamic? OK, we'll light up a fire for you. Abraham was put in the fire and the fire became coolness and safety for him, so we'll do the same with you and see. If it becomes coolness and safety then you really are Abrahamic!' Of course he didn't know what to do.

"Now I say the reconciling principle . . . but see how difficult it is to really understand the word. This can be perilous. For example, when Bush used the word 'crusade,' the whole world went up in arms over it, even though Al Gore had used the word during his campaign against Bush when Gore said that whoever is with us has to carry his cross and come. Gore was using this word against Bush, not against Muslims.

"Now I want to explain the perils of misunderstanding the meaning of a word like 'cross'. When Jesus said to his disciples, 'Whoever believes in me, let him take up his cross and follow me,' he means that whoever has possessions, let him leave them behind and follow me along the road of hardship, along the road of sacrifice. So the cross in the sight of Christ means firmness, it means to be steadfast in the face of temptations, it means to be rid of these temptations and to become sincere. The cross means the sincerity that is embodied in the sincere person.

"The one who saw this exact meaning is Imam Ali. During his time of great trial, his brother Aqeel wrote to ask about him. He replied to his brother's inquiry by saying, 'By God, Aqeel, I am as the poet said: If you ask me how am I? I am patient before the perils of time, a cross.' So the cross is the embodied sincerity of the sincere person who is steadfastly firm in the face of any temptation, in the face of any fear. That is the cross," Dr. Ali says emphatically. "The cross means that I am here to execute the will of the Father, I am here to execute my Father's will so I have to leave everything else aside. And Imam Ali gave clear meaning to this word by describing himself as a cross. I am a cross! Now every sincere person can use this word.

"Through historical contamination or literary contamination or contamination from certain events that distort common people's understanding, the cross came to mean enmity. Judaism came to mean enmity, as we just heard from Dr. Imran. But when we return to the purity of matters with understanding, we see that Jew means one who returns to his Rabb, as Moses returned and admonished Aaron and made him return to the certainty in God, not following the opinions of men, thus ridding the people of the idolatry of the golden calf and so on. Now these words have precious value; whenever we arrive at an understanding we solve a great problem in all the continents of the earth. The idea of the crusade for example—if the view of Imam Ali about being a cross were to be spread, matters would be very different. If we could spread the meaning of the staff, that would nullifiy sorcery. If we would spread the meaning of Judaism that returns us to God, that returns us to Hu, we would be rid of the problems that afflict people."

"You know I always have diverse people here, Armenian Christians, Sunnis, Shia, Jews, and so on. People ask me, what are these Armenians doing here? I tell them these Armenians are my Armenians. They ask me what are these Druze doing here? I tell them these Druze are my Druze. They ask me what are these Jews doing here? I tell them these Jews are my Jews. What I mean is that we are all originally the children of Adam. Fortunately for us some important things have come into being in the world, like the internet, satellites, TV and radio, so now one is able to obtain information and find things out in many ways. Take Afghanistan for instance. During Bin Laden's time we didn't know much about Afghanistan, but now this year I saw on satellite TV how the Afghanis are reviving the commemoration of Imam Hussein. I saw President Karzai speaking about Hussein and saying that everyone in Afghanistan, Shia and Sunni, commemorates his martyrdom. So I am approaching the subject of Afghanistan using communications from the media, so it is no longer the unknown Afghanistan of the hideouts and caves."

"Understanding is so important, so important. And understanding involves a thousand concerns, and each concern requires a thousand resolves. How many Iraqi satellite stations are there today?" Someone says there are seven or eight. "There are several stations transmitting to us news and knowledge," Dr. Ali continues. "We see many things, even crimes. Before this we couldn't see anything about Iraq. Now if we can also understand the meaning of words like 'cross,' or 'Jews,' or 'Islam' slowly and with deliberation . . . . You may argue yes, but there are wars in Palestine, in Iraq, in Ireland. I reply that this is correct, but what is your view? Do you have a view that can save us from this? Do you have a view that can extract us from such conflict? Tell us your view, but don't speak to us from the perspective of transgression and enmity, rather speak to us from the perspective of understanding."

Dr. Ali returns to the saying of Imam Ali, using his whole body to emphasize his message, "Right now I am considering Imam Ali's saying, 'If you ask me how I am, I am patient with the uncertainty of time, a cross.' I am explaining a piece of information that is of value about Imam Ali and his use of this word. He would not use a word that is filthy; this is a noble word. In other words, I am not presenting information for the sake of attacking someone, or to oppose someone. No, I present information for the sake of knowledge. If you ask me how I am, I am patient, patient." Dr. Ali is pounding his fist up and down for emphasis as he speaks. "Imam Ali distilled the whole story of Job with this saying. Patient is the last name in the Most Beautiful Names. God culminated all of His attributes with the Patient One. By speaking of the cross, Imam Ali emphasized the quality of patience, meaning 'I am immune, I am immune from temptations.'"

"I want to give another example of the cross. This second example is the cross of Muhammad. When his uncle, Abu Talib, came to him with the Meccan leaders' offer to make him their king and to give him whatever he desired of power, wealth, women, and so on in exchange for abandoning his prophetic mission, his answer was, 'By God, Uncle, if they place the sun in my right hand and the moon in my left hand in order to abandon this matter I will not leave it unless I perish.'" As Dr. Ali is saying this he stretches out his arms one by one to give the impression of being crucified. "And by saying this Muhammad went on to spread the message of Islam. So the cross is perseverance, it is firmness and strength."

Dr. Ali then smiles and tilts his head towards Kabir, "Now Kabir is probably saying to himself, 'What is happening with Asad Ali? He is speaking like the people of outward form. What's all this talk about history and language? Where did the Sufi go?'" He smiles broadly and gestures with his hand for us to wait, "The man is shocked, all I am talking about is history, law, language. Where is the dervish? Where is Mawlana?" he asks, laughing, "OK, here is something for your sake, for Caroleena's sake," he says, laughing with utter delight. "Crusader, Salibi, means Salli Bi, pray through me! pray through me. Just like Bismillah, Iqra' Bismi Rabbika," he says with emphasis on the Bi in these Quranic phrases. "Through God's power *pray*."

"Here's something from Tassawuf!" he says as he claps his hands and laughs. "Look at how many forms the cross has! Furthermore, the first one to use this word was Christ himself when one of the young men came to ask him how he could ascend to the highest dominion. Jesus gave him the Ten Commandments, but the young man protested that he already knew these things. So Jesus told him, 'Then sell everything that you possess and carry your cross and follow me!' The young man told him that he had much wealth and could not part with it, so he left. Jesus then said, 'It is easier for a camel to pass through the eye of the needle than for one who is attached to worldly wealth to enter heaven.' So the cross is Imam Ali. And it is Muhammad who is immune from the wealth of the whole world; it cannot tempt him.

"One of the declarations of Imam Ali is his saying, 'By God, even if I were given everything that is between heaven and earth in exchange for unjustly taking a husk of grain from an ant, I would not do it!' This is the cross, this is the cross; this is it! When Ahmad Imran made me cry, I was being shown the meaning of the cross. When he talked about the woman who asked Jesus to heal her sick child, he was talking about the use of the word Rabbunee by Jesus. When Jesus called out, Rabbunee, it was the same as Abraham's seeking protection from the fire. Would Jesus accept discriminating among people? Would he accept disappointing them? Would he refuse to help them? What can he do? What can he do?

"He was on the cross at that moment between his disciples and his understanding. This is why he said Rabbunee. He didn't say Ya Rabbi, he didn't say Father, he called out Rabbunee, meaning My Tender Rabb, and this brings a different understanding of everything. He made it clear that it is incumbent upon us to feed the dogs, it is incumbent upon us to heal the sick of all religions, it is incumbent upon us to work and act on the Sabbath, and on Sunday, and on Friday and every day! This is Rabbunee, Rabbunee; it's a nickname for Allah, but he used it to seek refuge in His Tenderness, that Rabb who is inside the membranes of our eyes, who is in our blood, who makes us see. This is the Rabb who carries you up to heaven and brings you back in a wink of an eye, this is Rabbunee!

"And this Rabbunee is the Rabb of the Cross, of steadfastness, of firmness. Just as we have, 'Say: I seek refuge in the Rabb of humanity, the Sovereign of humanity, the God of humanity,' seeking refuge in all these three at once, so seeking refuge in Rabbunee is the same as seeking these three. It's as if a child cries out to its mother, and even if she is angry with him once she hears his call to her, all burdens are lifted. Likewise, when Jesus cries out Rabbunee -ooh!, it has a great effect on me. This too is of Tassawuf. It's from the tears of Tassawuf, it is humility, it is gentleness, it is benevolence towards people. It is to return to the prevailing concepts and to breath new spirit into them, the spirit of understanding.

"In physics, Robert Oppenheimer said that the most difficult thing, the most serious thing, is to create the proper balance between superficiality and depth. This is the hardest thing and it is the thing we are in need of every day. Similarly, the Algerian author Malik Ibn Nabbi said that it was very difficult and very important to establish a balance between the learned idea of God and the marketplace idea of the masses about God. Just imagine how dangerous is the common idea that declares all people are infidels!" One of the women asks, 'Who says this?' and Dr. Ali responds, "Many a Mufti has said this! For example Sheikh Tantawi of Al Azhar when he was the Mufti of Egypt issued a fatwa based on the opinion of Ibn Taimiyya that was published in Al Ahram stating that all Shia factions are greater infidels than the Jews and Christians!"

This causes a reaction among some of the people in the gathering, "Who appointed him spokesman for God?" one of his nieces asks. "I am not speaking against the Mufti when I bring this up," Dr. Ali explains, "I am talking about the issue of understanding." The young niece asks, "Did he really mean it?" Dr. Ali smiles, "Yes and he even articulated practical action against the Shia. He proclaimed that their women can be taken captives and used as concubines! I am not saying anything against Sheikh Tantawi even though I responded to his fatwa in writing and told him that he does not represent any of the Muslims with this fatwa of his: 'It is true that you are the Mufti of Egypt but you represent no Muslims with such talk, you only represent your own five understandings. Our Islam is built upon five pillars while your ignorance is built upon five pillars: your ignorance of language, your ignorance of eloquence, your ignorance of history, your ignorance of philosophy, and your ignorance of the Quran itself!'

"The Quran says: To God prostrate everything in the heavens and earth. And Muhammad says: the closest a servant can come to his Rabb is when he is prostrate. This is the fatwa of Allah for His servants. Allah gave a fatwa to all His servants that they be close to Him, that they all serve Him and that they all worship Him. All that is in heavens and earth has surrendered to Him! This is the fatwa of Allah; this is the fatwa of Islam, whereas your fatwa represents your five ignorances. I do not wish to harm any Muslim with my words but my words are meant for you, Sheikh. Your ignorance led you to the words that you published in the public media. Don't think that I am against you, but I am against your method of understanding. When you say: Ibn Taimiyya said . . . and you depend on his opinion, well, we know him and we know what he stood for. He is long gone and so are the times in which he lived. I suggest that you try reading Surah Al Raad anew. This is the Surah that says: To God everything in the heavens and earth prostrates as well as their shadows . . . Even the shadows worship God! Nothing is excepted. My hands are obedient and the shadow of my hand is obedient.' I told him, 'If you can understand this Ayat, then I'll say: Peace be upon you, our Sheikh!' This incident first resulted in increased tension between Egypt and Syria, but it led to improved relations because Mubarak contacted Assad and tried to correct the situation and it led to dialogue and improvement in relations."

Another guest arrives, Sheikh Muhammad Badyani from Iran. After greetings and introductions, Dr. Ali turns to Kabir, "Going back to the issue of real meaning; such an understanding arises from the purification of concepts, and this causes wonders in this world. We believe this is the kind of understanding that is needed. Seeking understanding is what brings us together right now. Religions arose through understanding, through patience with concepts until they become clear. The incident with Sheikh Tantawi that I just told you had great benefit. The dialogue ended up moving him from his position. I told him I was amazed that the intelligent people of Egypt could make you their Mufti! Anyway he was moved to the position of Sheikh of Al Azhar, and as I mentioned, relations between the two countries grew and improved after this collision. May God bless him and grant him all goodness, how he's changed now! I never heard any other fatwa like that from him since that time.

"But if you only knew, if I were not a cross, I would have fallen into his temptations!" he says with amusement. "We return to say again that understanding is a thousand concerns and every concern requires a thousand resolves. Understanding is a grave responsibility.

How many sayings of the Prophet are there, how many examples are there in the Quran about this?" he asks.

Then turning his attention to our new guest he says, "Sheikh Badyani is one of our dear friends. He traveled through many areas of Syria and visited with several scholars and sheikhs to study the principles of the Shia. One time he came to visit me and he spent two hours with me. This visit made his mind whirl, just like Shamsuddin! There was a small booklet that clarified Sufi principles and the pure knowledge as it relates to the Alawis. This booklet was just nineteen pages. After these two hours he left and did not return until two years later. He resolved not to see me again until he had fully realized something that he now understood. When he returned to us he came with six volumes of work that explain the Gnostic principles of the Alawis. Doesn't he deserve a reward for this?" he asks Kabir, "Yes? What do you think, would Congress ratify this?" he asks jokingly of Kabir, "So in this way this Iranian sheikh became one of the doctors of creativity in our Union of Writers in Arabic."

"So when are we going to discuss your doctorate?" he asks Kabir, "here or in America? Or maybe in The Hague in the International Court of Justice? The Queen of Holland can grant it to you." Here Bassim interjects, "You like the Queen of Holland very much." Dr. Ali nods, "Yes, by God I do. I really appreciate her. I spoke about her two or three times on Syrian Satellite TV. She has some great stands on issues. For example, she will not accept unresolved conflict within her realm. One time the deviant Muslims and the Sufis had a conflict and she told the Sufi sheikhs that they had to either resolve their conflict with the deviant Muslims or leave Holland. So the Sufi Sheikh ascended the pulpit and said to the radicals: Brother, may God help you and strengthen you! This is a great matter indeed. This matter resembles the spirit of Surah Al Kafirun; you have your religion and I have my religion. Imagine this! God with the tongue of His prophet made the infidelity of the deniers a religion! He didn't insult them or ridicule them. Imagine this respect, even for the beliefs of people like these. This is democracy, this is the democracy of the People of the Household (Prophet Muhammad and his family).

"But let us return to the question of understanding. I went into seclusion on the first day of Muharram and just came out today. During all that time neither Hussein nor Christ allowed me to participate in any public commemoration of Ashura. I was occupied with the presence of Christ and Hussein together. I listened and heard from them and I wrote a book about their meeting together and how they talked together. And what is the reconciling principle between them? It is sacrifice.

"We don't want just talk. We don't want acting. We want practical, effective action. Here is Kabir Helminski from California in America; he wants to know, and he wants to transmit knowledge, so he brings himself all the way from America and honors us here. He gives matters their proper due. It is not like someone who lives right here next to me who tells me: Oh I am really busy, I have company and I can't attend your talk today. So here is practical action, the reconciling principle. Christ, he is the reconciling principle: sacrifice. Hussein, he is the reconciling principle: sacrifice. I sacrifice myself for the world. I sacrifice myself for my grandfather's community. They did as they said; the reconciling princple is action, action, action.

"The principle is not just letters. If you take the word HARF in Arabic and read it from the other direction it is FARAH, or joy. The word is not meant to deaden. Christ says the letter slays, but the spirit brings to life. The spirit is the heart, when you revert to it, you find joy. In the teachings of religious law, Sharia . . . you know, people imagine that because we are Sufis that we have abandoned Sharia, but this is not correct. In our view Sharia is the source of happiness. How? It's letters are SH-R-`A if you enter from its heart (the inverse) it becomes `ARSH, or Throne. This means Sharia carries you to the Throne which encompasses the heavens and earth. This is for today. Entering into the heart is essential," he says in a low voice as he reflects upon the words.

Then turning to Sheikh Badyani he smiles and says, "You have good luck with Americans! He is Iranian and the last time he was here we had another American guest, Mr. Brian Cox also from California, and they were very happy to meet each other, and we had an Iraqi with us too. He was delightted. Iraq, Iran and America together! This is Abrahamic, this is Abrahamic! But we don't know who is who, the Abrahamics are the Musawis (of Moses), the Issawis (of Jesus), and Muhammadis (of Muhammad). I think the Iranians are the Musawis because Ayatollah Khomeini used to refer to himself as Ruhullah Al Musawi."

As one of the guests, Ma`an Ali, gets up to leave we also get up to say goodbye and Dr. Ali recounts a story about him. "When I was a nursing infant, his grandfather, who was my mother's relative, came to visit, and my mother asked him to give me my name. Now his grandfather was Sheikh Asad Ali, a great scholar and astronomer. Well, he told my mother that my name was Kamil. My mother told me that as soon as she started calling me Kamil, I cried, and when she tried to nurse me I refused. So I remained on civil strike, crying and refusing to nurse until his grandfather's sheikh, whose name was Habib Eid, came and placed his index finger between my eyes and said to my mother, 'No your son's name is not Kamil, his name is Asad.' And I accepted that I was Asad (happiest), not Kamil (complete). This is why I seek the Kamils (the complete ones) because I am incomplete. If I were Kamil, everyone would be after me; no it is better for me to continue seeking knowledge, to stay incomplete, so that I will always be seeking completion. His grandfather put me on the cross. I continue to think about The Complete One. It is true I am incomplete, but I keep asking how the human being can become complete?"

"How many letters did you write me, do you remember?" Dr. Ali asks Kabir after we sit down to resume our conversation. "Maybe fifteen," Kabir answers.

"I have a book of Imam Ali in which I've put one of your letters. Let me show it to you," he says as he gets up to fetch it. "This is the fifth volume of the interpretation of Imam Ali's *Nahj Al Balagha* by the title *The Structures of the Ideal Republic*," Dr. Ali says as he returns with the book. He then proceeds to describe the cover illustration done by Dr. Ali Himdan of a peacock, a falcon and a tree—representing Imam Ali's book of wisdom, Imam Ali himself and Dr. Ali, his interpreter. He calls that cover the Eastern side, the one in Arabic. He then flips the book to its other side, the Western side, in English and reads, "Imam Ali and His Wisdoms," and he goes through the same title in five different Western languages. "The first page of the Western side, now don't tell anyone because it's a secret, but look —whose signature is this?" he asks with a broad smile as he hands the open book to Kabir, "Read for us with your own voice," he commands.

Kabir reads aloud the letter he wrote years ago. "Beloved Asad Ali . . . .." At this point Dr. Ali addresses me, "Abu Eid, now I don't know what he says in this letter, so if he's saying bad things about me I want you to tell me, OK?" He breaks out in his delightful laughter, "If there are insults in this letter you'll uncover them for me today!" he continues to joke. Kabir laughs and reads on, "Thank you for speaking directly to my soul. I will try to deserve and use the gifts that you so generously offered us. Our days here are very intense and full. I wish to remember to be grateful for everything. And through these days I am thankful that I have your example to inspire me. You seem to know my heart as well as it knows itself or more." Dr. Ali interrupts my translation saying, "More, more!" I nod my head, realizing that he doesn't really need my translation.

Kabir continues, "What can I say except Shukr Lillah? Here at last are the pictures you said Nuha needed. I still hope it will be possible to return with Camille and maybe Cara within one year. With my greatest gratitude, respect and love." Dr. Ali leans forward, "What was the date?" he asks. "August 14th 1996," Kabir responds reopening the book and looking at Dr. Ali. "So in 1996 he says they want to return after a year with Cara. How many years have passed since? This is an American promise," he says with a dismissive gesture of the hand and breaks out laughing again and we all join him.

"It wasn't a promise, it was a wish," I say trying to defend my

Sheikh, but Dr. Ali's attention is on the book and he doesn't hear me. "Here is another letter from one of Sheikh Kabir's students, Gaston Fontaine. Would you like to see it?" He hands the book back to Kabir. "I know this one," Kabir says. "Still, read it with your voice," Dr. Ali directs. "Dear Dr. Ali, please find enclosed the Chilean version of your new *Opening Surah*. Thank you very much for giving me the opportunity to work with it. I asked my Arabic teacher to translate it to Spanish, and I worked on his translation and on the original English one to produce two modified versions. I like it very much and working with it has given me the chance to understand it better. This is the kind of work I love doing and, inshallah, I will continue doing it whenever I have the chance to do it. If you feel that I could help with this kind of work for you please let me know and I will gladly do my best to be of service. I want to ask your help in order to be able to meet you in the Inner Garden of Paradise."

"How do you like that, what a simple request this is!" Dr. Ali exclaim, laughing, "Just give me your hand and pull me up to the Inner Garden of Paradise. Yes!" Kabir goes on to read the last part of Gaston's letter: "And if you can extend your hand and continue helping me I would be so grateful. I hope you've received the pictures. Please receive all my love and gratitude. P.S. I read your *New Opening Surah* to my wife yesterday and she liked it very much and asked for a copy of it."

Dr. Ali responds by saying, "Very sweet, delightful. He has a very good style of writing too. He wrote to me in Spanish and you can find it in the book, *For Adam's Sake*. How is he now?" Dr. Ali inquires.

"I haven't heard very much from Gaston for a few years, as far as I know everything is good," Kabir replies. "He is from Santiago?" Dr. Ali asks, "His relationship with you is special, he wrote me another letter telling me about how he saw images which, as you had explained to him, meant the straight path to Allah. I mean it is not right that Fontaine should be abandoned as long as he thinks this way about you. You should ask about him," he says to Kabir with a searching tone.

"He's been with another teacher in Turkey and his focus is a little bit more in that direction," Kabir explains. "This should not be a limitation," Dr. Ali says, "So that the words will remain, so that the relations will continue, sometimes I use these letters in my books to refer to the network," he explains, "because you are all schools, every one of you." "You connect the wires. Even when they get disconnected you reconnect them," Kabir says humbly.

"There is another fellow by the name of Hatem, a Tunisian," Dr. Ali continues, "Yes, we know Hatem," Kabir responds.

"He wrote a letter, not to me, but to someone else here by the name of Ahmad Hussein," Dr. Ali continues. "It was a very delicious letter; besides being truthful it was also delicious. In the letter to Ahmad Hussein, well, he's gossiping about me behind my back," he says jokingly, "Ahmad Hussein is one of the people in Damascus who see in their dreams a certain person," he says, pointing to himself. "And he receives lessons from him in his dreams. So he writes to Ahmad saying I met a group of people—referring to you, Kabir—who are friends of your teacher and in my opinion are the most refined learning society in America. They are the Everest of learning in America. I liked what Hatem said very much, although he didn't write it to me directly, but wrote it to me behind my back!"

He opens the book that Kabir was reading from once again and says, "Here is the Ayat. 'And He caused affection between their hearts' is written in several languages. This is our slogan: Affection. In how many languages is this said? We have it in 24 languages plus Arabic which corresponds to the number of prophets mentioned in the Quran."

He then leans forward and pointing with his index finger asks, "What important news or work do you have now?" Kabir replies, "Just this week I was asked by a major publisher to rewrite a book about Islam. Inshallah, to breathe some life into a book that needs some life." Dr. Ali nods in agreement, "New spirit, splendid." "The idea that's burning in me . . .." Kabir begins, but is interrupted by

Dr. Ali. "It pleases me much that they are discovering you! They conducted a war in Iraq to discover WMD and after four years of searching they discovered nothing. This means you are more power-ful than the WMD's!" he says laughing. Kabir tries again, "The idea that's burning in me, and which you have contributed to tonight, is the idea of writing a book called *Creative Islam*, because so much of what we see in the name of Islam, and especially in the West, is not creative. If we could reveal the creative power of Islam, this would be good." Dr. Ali responds in agreement, "As the late blessed Annemarie Schimmel said, if Westerners could see the creative pow-er of Islam they would love the essential nature of Islam."

"And another project is that we've just moved to a new home and center." Dr. Ali immediately asks, "And what is it's name?" Kabir continues, "It's a Spanish name, Casa Paloma, the House of the Dove." Dr. Ali repeats, "The dove! Nice." Kabir continues, "It's a beautiful place, it has a fountain and a courtyard . . .."

Dr. Ali interrupts, "I am waiting for permission from . . ." and he points with his finger upwards. Kabir continues, "It has two houses and a meeting place which is a yurt. And from this land you can see the ocean." Dr. Ali smiles, "O Peace, O Peace, how tempting!" he exclaims and laughs, "I am patient with the uncertainty of times, a cross!" he exclaims.

Kabir continues, "If you want to see an earthly reflection of Jannah, come to Casa Paloma. It was interesting because when we were buying the property there were many stages of bargaining and negotiations, but the day the deed was recorded was the day of the Urs of Mawlana Jalālu'ddin Rūmī."

Dr. Ali raises his head, "That day you called me, the three of you," he says, "That day I was remembering you and I told you that I had something very special for you." He then gets up and asks us to go with him to the dining room. There on the bookshelves he points to a row of books, each bound in light green covers with a white dove. "The dove is the symbol of Fatima," Dr. Ali tells us pointing to the books, "Fatima, the Radiant! Do you see the connection, the bond that is between us?" We gather beneath the books and take some photographs. Soon it's time for us to go back to the hotel; it's a short time till dawn.

As we get ready to sleep in our room, I sit down with my journal to write down my thoughts about the evening. Understanding; this was a key message for us tonight. I reflect on what was said and what took place during the sohbet of Dr. Ali, our living Mawlana. To me, Asad Ali is proof of the Universal, Complete Human Being, Al Insan Al Kamil. The first time I met him I was overwhelmed by his presence and his unique use of language. This time I am able to understand more clearly what he stands for, what his meaning is in this world. He is the human being transcendent beyond the bounds that hold us back from spiritual freedom, from true faith. He is beyond doctrine, beyond sectarianism, beyond nationalism, beyond religion as we commonly know it. He is Tawheed in its human form; he is a human being who can embrace all of humanity with all of its beauty, all of its creativity, and all of its limitations and failings within his heart. He is a human being who sees with certainty the unifying and integrating meanings of the expressions of divine love in the words of all faiths. He is proof of the tremendous power of humility, and he is proof of the irresistible force of love. His being is the clear evidence of the Nafs that has been tamed by love and is at peace within the embrace of its Rabb. And he is living proof of how the Nafs that is tamed by love is filled with happiness, laughter, receptivity and presence.

Reflecting on my impressions I see how I reacted negatively to Dr. Imran. I saw that he was mainly interested in expressing his views and was not very attentive to Dr. Ali's teachings. I saw him waiting for an opening to say things, I saw him talking about things that were not relevant to the discussion, and I saw him trying to teach Dr. Ali about such elementary things that I considered his behavior to be poor Adab, to lack proper respect. He was in the circle of a master and yet all he wanted to do was talk.

Then I thought about Dr. Ali and how attentive he was to Dr.

Imran, even though Dr. Imran was interrupting him and saying things that were out of place. I could see that he was amused most of the time by the things that his guest was saying. He did not react in any way that would offend or hurt Dr. Imran. I could see that Dr. Ali truly held him in high regard. He honored him even though he was acting improperly, and he received from him a very special gift, the meaning of Rabbunee, even though Dr. Imran mentioned it in a completely different context and was talking about a completely different topic. Yet that one word and the story of its utterance was the central message of the sohbet.

I learned something very important from this. I learned how we cannot receive anything when we are judging others. When we are negatively evaluating people's behavior, all we can see is what they are doing that is not right. Dr. Ali on the other hand was beyond judging. He was open and receptive to everyone in his presence. He interacted with each one of us as a valuable jewel, as a worthy child of Adam, and so he received. He received and he shared with us a precious gift of understanding and wisdom. I see how I am veiled by my senses and my ego from the truth and I ask Allah to remove these veils from my heart.

I think back on the evening and see how Dr. Ali was addressing us directly with his words. He spoke of endurance, constancy, perseverance, staying the course in the face of trials and hardships so that one can reach the heights of excellence. He was showing us our sporadic actions, our lack of focus and inconstancy. I think about how it's been seven years since the gift of Chapter 366 of Ibn Arabi's *Futuhat* ("On the Spiritual Qualities of the Helpers of the Mahdi") was given to Kabir and to me. Until now we haven't completed its work, we haven't yet fully received its meaning, and we haven't yet drunk its water. I wonder how I became distracted for seven years. How could so much time pass without action on my part? Last time Dr. Ali made it clear that he wanted us to work on translating more of the poems from *The Lights of the Quran* into English. We didn't do it; we were busy with everything else and took nothing of what he gave us. Seven years, seven years, how strange! I ask Allah to forgive me for my heedlessness and I ask for guidance and resolve so that I do not fall into this trap of neglect again. It's almost dawn now; I'll wait to offer Fajr prayer before going to sleep. I close my journal and stretch out on the bed. I look to my right and see that Kabir is asleep. I feel blessed to be here.

Damascus Night 2

Wednesday February 23, 2005

We are in the living room waiting for Dr. Ali to appear. Soon he enters, dressed in white robes with a gold trim on his outer cape. He seems to appear out of nowhere and to be standing before us like an apparition. As we get up to greet him he gestures with his hand for us to sit and begins to recite a quatrain:

> *Like Solomon and his father,*
> *A Messiah lives in accordance with the one who seeks him.*
> *The verdancy of the Ever-Living One is in our form.*
> *Adam is alive in his progeny.*

مِثلَ سليمانُ و والِدِهِ

عاش مسيحٌ وَفقَ قاصِدِهِ

خُضرَةُ الحيِّ بقالَبِنا

آدمُ حيٌّ في موالِدِهِ

Then he sits down in his chair and smiles at us as he directs us to repeat the quatrain one by one around the room.

"The Quran is complete. Some people say that the Quran needed completion because the Arabs used to write without dots or diacritical marks, and Hajjaj completed it later with his dots! This is just some talk, but now for us . . . ." he trails off as he returns to the first line of the quatrain, *Like Solomon and his father.* "This line is a key that takes us to all the places of Solomon and David. This is a prototype of Solomon's mission in the Quran. What is the mission of Solomon in the Quran? It is to spread Islam among the Arabs!" he announces with delightful laughter, as he claps his hands together for emphasis.

"This is the Jewish prophet. People don't understand that the word 'Jew' (Yahud) means to return to God."

Someone asks why he's bringing this up now and he explains that this is what is required at the present moment. He turns to Kabir and says, "You have to reach many different people—English, American, European. You have to confront strange and amazing things, you have to confront a broad spectrum from Bush to . . . who is this famous American woman who dances around a lot?" "Brittney Spears?" I offer. "No, not her," he says and keeps looking around for someone to name her. "Madonna," one of his young nieces says finally. "Yes, Madonna! You have to strive between Bush and Madonna," he tells Kabir with a laugh. "And you have to keep whirling like a Mawlawi!" he continues with increasing laughter. "This is why you need to hear this. This is your weapon. These are our weapons; these are our fleets. We have only that which brings to life the dead heart, just as Jesus did, or which awakens a queen like Bilqis, a queen of Arabs, who has the readiness to ascend to heaven. This is how the Messiah spoke of her in the Bible; the Queen of the South ends up in heaven and she will continue the generation of the Messiah because she loves wisdom and turns towards it wherever it may be.

"Of course when the Messiah said these words, he meant them for every woman who turns towards wisdom and who accords with the voice of God and is thus a queen in the view of Jesus. And she ends up in heaven, meaning that she is of benefit on earth and in heaven. She is one of the hosts of God, who is given sovereignty on earth and who is given authority in heaven. So, *like Solomon and his father,* these are keys with which we can see the realms displayed before us of the wisdom of Solomon and David. What did these human beings do according to the Quran? What was the work of Solomon among the Arabs?

"Now the second line, *A Messiah lives in accordance with the one who seeks him.* Now what corresponds to this line? For the first line, we found the correspondance in Surah Al Nahl regarding Solomon.

54

So what is the Surah that matches this second line about the Messiah? Which Surah shows us how Jesus lived? It is Maryam, right? Surah Maryam is what corresponds to this line. Jesus is mentioned in the Quran seventy-two times, sometimes as Jesus, at other times as Messiah, and at other times as Son of Mary. Messiah is mentioned twenty-five times and there are also twenty-five prophets mentioned in the Quran."

Someone in the circle (a doctor who specializes in natural medicines) says, "I've discovered a secret!" Dr. Ali enthusiastically replies, "Please, tell us about it." The man explains, "The quatrain is made up of fourteen words and the total number of its letters is fifty eight. If we add them the sum is seventy two!"

Just then new guests arrive, a husband and wife, and the conversation takes a different turn, "Welcome, come in," says Dr. Ali. "This is Dr. Zakaria Mir Alam. He is an MP in the Syrian parliament; he is Abu Yahya (father of John), and this is Umm Yahya (mother of John). She is one of the 'doctors of creativity.' He is Zakaria and Zakaria is my greatest of trials," Dr. Ali says, "because every week, three times each week I undertake the practice of Zakaria (three days of silence). But thanks to this practice there have come many fruits, because at the end of each three days a Yahya is born to me; that one who cannot be imitated, that one who is neither of East nor West.

"Today we are more in the West than in the East, or more like the West. In my father's will and testament he wrote to me, 'Read Surah Al Araaf and do not forget the Noble Ones (the Prophet's family) and I expect from you the East in the eye of the West, meaning that the sun is to rise in the West. And here are our suns rising in the West! I am fulfilling the will of my highest Father as well when I read the Quran. So don't any of you get too conceited! I am only fulfilling the will of the Father and my father. I am not doing it for anyone else's sake!" he exclaims, and breaks out laughing with delight.

Mawlana Asad then turns his attention back to the doctor, who repeats his insight about the numerical connection of the quatrain with the Messiah's mention in the Quran. Then he says, "It's been five years since Kabir came here." Dr. Ali says to Kabir, "I never 'remember' you, because I never forget you. Since we've come to know Kabir, I would say, tens or maybe hundreds of times the mention of East and West is made in our gatherings, and always the address of the West for us is Kabir Helminski. So he has made his imprint upon us here. And my brothers here are my witnesses to the truth of this. Besides, Mahmoud came with us that one time to the University of Damascus and saw for himself how well known Kabir is among our students. The reason really is that Jesus, Son of Mary, gave all this to him the same way he gave it to the Queen of the South, because of his love of knowledge."

He then leads us in reciting the rest of the quatrain. After Kabir finishes reciting, Mawlana exclaims, "Well, now Kabir is speaking Arabic and reciting quatrains! This is Moses' staff, he's going to walk out of here singing tonight!" Kabir picks up on the merriment, "Tell him we'll set it to music as soon as we get home."

Dr. Ali concurs. "Yes, it's a lyrical poem. What is important is that our interaction and relationship with the Quran is a great matter. The Quran in fact truly heals and it brings to life the dead earth, and it moves the mountains that people imagine are stationary, but definitely only 'in accordance with' (bi wifq). Now I really want you to understand the meaning of this word Wifq (in accordance with), because this word has to do with alignment of the constellations and with the synchronizing of days so conception can occur . . .." As I listen to him a word comes into my heart to capture this meaning, "Resonance . . . resonance with," I say to Kabir. "Very good, I like this word very much, resonance," Dr. Ali says pronouncing it in French, "because I find the sound of the stars within it."

Now he turns to his niece, Nedda, who has translated the quatrain into English, and asks her to read it. When she recites it Dr. Ali says, "Good, now we want to produce a new translation for this quatrain for the sake of establishing a foundation, in order to connect it with the Quran, and so we will recognize that the Quranic words are heavenly (falakiyya). For example, it says in Al Waqi'ah: I vow by the *places of the stars. And truly it is indeed a great vow if only you knew! It is truly a noble recital in a book that is hidden like a pearl that cannot be touched except by those who are purified, a bestowal from the Lord of the Worlds.*

"Now what is the relationship between the places of the stars and the Noble Quran? What's the story here, what's going on, eh?" he asks, as Kabir reads English translations of the Ayats from the Quran. "*Only the pure ones shall touch it.* What is the relationship? Now I am asking the East for the sake of the West: what is the relationship between an artist, and his painting?" Dr. Ali (speaking to Ali Hamdan, the artist) says, "What is the relationship of the places of the stars with the purified Quran which can only be touched by the pure ones? We have a painting here but it is God who is its artist. Why is He vowing by that which none can see? The Earth is but a head of a pin compared to the places of the stars, so what is the relationship between the structure of the universe and God telling us that only the pure can touch the Quran? What is the composition of this painting? We have stars in the heaven and verses in the Quran, what is the connection?"

Kabir responds, "When the sun rises the stars disappear." Dr. Ali listens and then breaks into laughter, "With us there is no setting! No setting, no setting! The people of Shamsuddin Tabrizi do not set, they are not absent. We want to paint a canvas now. So we have the great American space telescope Hubble; it is taking pictures of countless galaxies and there are several observatories on earth also photographing the places of the stars. With each new discovery in space we find that our previous knowledge of the universe is as small as an olive pit! And the expanses of the stars are ever-expanding, so the more we explore, the more wonders we see. This is why the Quran tells us, *And truly it is indeed a great vow if only you knew!* Listen to the structure of the words, listen . . . *if you only knew*, if you only understood the meaning of these words. All these galaxies that are made known to us show us the greatness of the Creator through His Creation."

Now a bemused smile appears on Dr. Ali's face, and holding

back his laughter he says, "The ancient geniuses used to track camels by examining their dung, so they said, 'The dung is the indication of the camel!'" He tilts his head up and breaks into a loud laughter as he waits for me to translate this aphorism. "These galaxies make apparent to us the greatness of God the All-Encompassing One. *It is truly a noble Quran.* Here is the greater of the Two Momentous Things that Prophet Muhammad mentioned in his saying, *'I leave with you the two momentous things, the greater of which is the Quran and the second is the guidance of the people of my household.'* Also, *It is truly a noble recital in a book that is hidden (Maknun) like a pearl. Maknun* means concealed. No matter how much you may fathom of it, it is still unknown. Look at us here on earth: this whole planet earth is nothing but a head of a pin compared to one galaxy that we see with the Hubble telescope."

At this point Kabir asks a question, "Why does it say that it is a Quran *in a hidden book?*" Dr. Ali listens intently. "Ah, good, very good. First of all the Noble Quran, which is more generous than the generosity of any human being in its bounteous giving, is a word like *A Messiah lives in accordance with the one who seeks him* meaning in accordance with its generosity. But *In a hidden book* refers to a particular code which we sometimes call The Preserved Tablet, and sometimes The Hidden Book. For example you come to Damascus and you bring a map of all the holy places which shows you where to go, but the Hidden Book holds the key, the indication of how to read it.

"You can know that *Maknun* means it holds universes within it. In order to reach these galaxies and to be able to read the places of the stars you have to find the hidden book. When you search for the hidden book in the Quran, you will find descriptions of it—for example, in the Surahs that begin with Ha Mim, but *only the pure ones can touch it. Maknun* means the veiled universes, or the universes that are indicated in these words. These words are like shells that hold meaning. For example, 'Kabir' is a word, but it is a shell. If there is a large crowd of people and I call out 'Kabir,' you will appear to me from among this crowd. The letters that make up this word are the shell and Kabir is the person, the one who is living who is indicated by this word. This is the pearl that is hidden inside the letters K–B–R.

"So here is the connection between the places of the stars and the Noble Quran that is in the state of constant generous giving, with the condition that one approaches it in accordance, in resonance with the hidden book. This discourse is impossible for anyone to grasp unless they are in a state of complete and total purity in body, thoughts, emotions, and intention. These four parts are the cornerstones of the real Kaaba. This is the Kaaba of purity—that you become pure in your body, pure in your thoughts, pure in your emotions, and pure in your intentions. And then your aim can be like a mother, producing a birth—the way that Jesus came into being in response to the intention of his mother. We call the Hidden Book the 'Mother of the Book.' That is, the Quran is contained in the Mother of the Book. *God effaces and affirms and with Him is the Mother of the Book*—meaning that from Him comes the aim, the meaning of the book."

We pause as tea is served and then Dr. Ali continues. "Have you ever visited the Himalayas?" he asks Kabir with a playful look. When Kabir shakes his head he asks incredulously, "You've never climbed Everest?" Kabir laughs and Dr. Ali cries out, "Who has climbed Everest here, young men and women? In the sohbet you climbed up, eh?" he says with a chuckle. "Well, if we cannot climb up to the peak of Everest, then what about the places of the stars? OK, what is the highest waterfall in the world?" he asks. In response Niagara, Victoria and other names are mentioned. Finally Dr. Ali Hamdan gives the correct answer: the Angel Falls in Venezuela. "Yes it's almost a kilometer high, which makes it nearly twenty times higher than Niagara Falls. So the highest mountain is Everest and the highest falls are Angel. In the book *Woman and Truth,* we presented these two heights as analogies for them. Everest is the woman and Angel is the truth. The rock and the water, the rock and the water—here are the true heights, here are the true heights.

"So why do we say 'Glory to God the Most High' when we pray, when we prostrate? We do this so He will take us up to the places of the stars, and to make us understand the relationship between the organization and order of the Ayats of the Quran and the arrangement of the places of the stars. The Quran is a map containing waterfalls and summits and valleys and deserts and depths with treasures in these depths and oceans and civilizations beneath these oceans, and so on and on. The Quran is discovered with the same precision and science with which we discover the places of the stars. And this is why we say:

> *Like Solomon and his father,*
> *A Messiah lives in accordance with the one who seeks him.*
> *The verdancy of The Ever-Living One is in our form.*
> *Adam is alive in his progeny.*

"These words are simple. Where is the piece of paper on which they are written? If we take the first and third lines, they are made of three Arabic words each, so three and three together form what? Thirty three. Now let's take the second and fourth lines, they are made of four words each, so four and four together form what? They are forty four and that is the number of Surah Maryam, according to the order of its revelation. So forty four is Maryam and thirty three is the age of Jesus and this makes the quatrain Jesus Son of Mary," he exclaims, laughing with relish, "This is the quatrain. And if we want to learn languages we need Jesus, Son of Mary. We can't travel without Jesus because he is the Word and the Spirit.

"Sheikh Kuftaro, the late Mufti of Syria, may God have mercy on his soul, used to say, 'I cannot be a Muslim unless I read Surah Maryam and Al Imran,' meaning, I want Jesus. We say Gabriel is the Holy Spirit and this is why the Noble Quran solves the whole theological problem for us and takes us into the knowledge of the All-Encompassing One, to the places of the stars in the words of God. This is why it says this is a great vow if only you knew. If you just know the code you will understand. This is why it says that the Gnostics are the ones who are most in awe of God. And this is why Imam Ali said, 'I've never argued with a Gnostic without prevailing upon him and I've never argued with an ignoramus without being prevailed upon."

Dr. Ali then asks Kabir to read the translation of the last part of these ayats, "Only the clean shall touch it." Kabir recites from the English translation. "What do you think about this, is this a correct translation?" he asks us. "Does someone understand the Quran by touching the book with his finger?" he asks with a laugh as he places his index finger on the Quran. "No, this is not a correct translation," he pronounces. "Anyone can take the Quran and tear it up if they want to. The Quran is not understood by physical touch. I want to really convey the idea here. Prophet Abraham is very concerned today about him, he wants to teach him Arabic and to teach him interpretation and to teach him how to touch the Quran," he says— apparently talking about Kabir.

"This Quran that is realized in the places of the stars is arranged with the same geometry as the stars. God who engineered the universe has engineered the words of this Quran. And it is impossible to see space without an instrument like Hubble; you know Hubble is a Sheikh! He helps us to see, to know, to sense with the spirit, not with the fingers. So, we ask God, the Exalted, to grant you purity so that you will touch the Noble Quran and you will know the greatness of the places of the stars. It is not just an idle vow. God vows in order to teach us. It is truly a marvel."

Damascus Night 3

A healer through abundance (Kawthar), the one of the lights heals me,
and Saleh through the seven binary opposites gives me to drink.
Allah is Light and is the Bestower. His smiles are like an olive,
the camel of the signs brings me to life.

"What relationship do we have with Rumī?" Dr. Ali asks us, as our third
evening with him begins. "Badiuzaman Foruzanfar is considered the
foremost interpreter of Jalālu'ddin Rumī. He produced twelve volumes
about Rumī. But unfortunately he doesn't like Muḥyīuddīn Ibn Arabi!"
he says with a chuckle. "I like Sheikh Muḥyīuddīn, so I asked him why
he doesn't like him and he told me he just doesn't, he likes Jalālu'ddin.
He was my advisor for my doctoral work, 'Art and Gnosis'. When I was
defending my thesis he wanted to take it to look at it, but I wouldn't
let him. He was of penetrating intelligence and he understood that I
wouldn't let him touch my work because I thought he could not sense
the meaning of my work. I was talking about Rumī when he suddenly
interrupted me with 'Ah, you said Ushq!'

"I told him that if he heard me say this then I did say it. 'You said
Ushq not Ishq.' He repeated. He called for a dictionary and looked up
the word, and it was Ishq. He called for another dictionary and another
and all of them said Ishq. 'Young man, you said Ushq and all the Arabic
dictionaries say Ishq!' He wanted to exact revenge from me for not let-
ting him look at my work. In the world of spirit, in my unseen world,
I started calling Rasul Allah, because in Iran they used to say to me that
I was the son of Rasul Allah. So I was beseeching Him in my secret to
please save me from the bind I was in with my professor! I didn't want
to be the Arab who does not speak correctly before him. Suddenly my
heart opened up and the answer came to me. So I opened my eyes and
said to him, 'Yes it is Ushq. This is what I said.' But he protested that all
the Arabic dictionaries say Ishq. 'All the dictionaries are wrong,' I told

him," he recalls, laughing,

"Now at that time I was just a young student and entirely under his authority. He said to me, 'It is so strange, sir. How can you say such a thing?' So I asked him whether Umar Ibn Rabia was an erotic poet, and he said, yes, he was indeed. So what word did he use for his love for women? He said immediately, 'Ishq,' So I told him that Jalālu'ddin Rumī and Muhyiuddīn Ibn al ʿArabī and all the other Sufis talk about love for God, so shall we call this Ishq too? Is love of God the same as earthly love? He said, no. So I told him that what is for the lower world is said with the sound of "i" [in "ishq"] (indicated by a diacritical mark below the letter) and what is for the higher world is made with the sound of "u" [in "ushq"] (indicated by a diacritical mark above the letter). This is why for Rumī it's Ushq and for Ibn Rabia it's Ishq! And at this explanation Foruzanfar exclaimed, 'Subhanallah, subhanallah! You are our master, sir! You are our master! We are truly amazed by your eloquence.' So you see what we mean now about the weave of heaven and the places of the stars, the places of the Ayats, the places of the Nafs, meaning the connection between the selves.

"Badiuzaman Foruzanfar loves Rumī. Kabir loves Rumī and also loves Ibn Arabi, even though Kabir's tradition is from Rumī. I have combined Rumī and Ibn Arabi, since both are beloved to me. And now I have both the school of Rumi and the school of Ibn Arabi in America. In Berkeley there is the Ibn Arabi Society which commemorates Ibn Arabi every year. And in Washington, Hammil named her home The Ibn Arabi House.

"What I want to communicate is how the places of the stars can be read in the Ayats of the Quran and the Ayats can be read in the positions of the stars on the pathways of the heavens. Also, relationships between people can be read in accordance with the places of the stars, in accordance with, in resonance with, the places of the stars. The Quran brings together the horizons and the selves and considers these two paths to Truth.

"*We shall show them Our signs on the horizons and in their selves until it becomes evident to them that He (It) is the Truth*" he recites from the Quran, as he hands it to Kabir to read the English translation. Then he says, "Our Master Abraham commanded us to take special care of Kabir today! I saw him today and he gave me special instructions for his sake." He continues, "Consider how amazing it is how our relationship with each other came into being. What brought us together? It is God who made the heaven's pathways, its cables and lines that are all interconnected, so that he made the stars bring one person to know another and so on, in order that Truth may become manifest to us. All the signs, the Quran, the stars, our souls—everything affirms one thing in the end: The Truth (Al Haqq).

"At the top, at the summit, why do we say 'Glory be to God the Most High,' why? Because when we remember the Most High we are closest to Him, the Most High. The Prophet said, 'The closest a servant is to his Lord is when he is prostrate.' From this idea came the summit or top. The seventh heaven is known as Tuba. In Surah Al Raad, which is the neighbor of Abraham, this is mentioned: *Those who have attained faith and whose hearts find tranquility through remembrance of Allah.* Indeed, it is through Allah's remembrance that hearts become tranquil. For those who have attained to faith and do good deeds there is bliss (Tuba) and a beautiful return. Tuba is the seventh heaven; Firdaus (Paradise) is the third heaven. These words of the Quran are precise and profoundly deep.

"The translators use 'Paradise' but there are actually seven different heavens. There is Eden (Adan), there is Repose (Qarar), there is Paradise (Firdaus), there is Bounty (Naim), there is Immortality (Khulud), there is the Abode (Ma'awa), and then there is Bliss (Tuba). Jesus says, know the Truth and Truth will set you free. It is through purity that we can traverse in an instant the light years from one heaven to the next."

At this point someone asks about the spirit and the heart. "The heart is a container, a mold, a place, an airport, it is art: HE-ART. Whereas the spirit is living, it is life in this atmosphere. When you turn the word spirit (RUH) over in Arabic it becomes HUR. Spirit is a word with a single meaning on the surface, but when you enter into the inner meanings, you find that it is many words, many states.

"Do you know what HUR means?" he asks, and someone gives the usual answer about the beautiful women of Paradise. "No, no," Dr. Ali replies. "HUR, which is the heart of the spirit, means the divine capacities that form the Most Beautiful Names and what is manifest through them in this world. It is the expansive divine capacities. We see a star and it looks like a small dot, but when you come near it you see how tremendous it is! So this is why I love both Muhyīuddīn and Jalālu'ddin. They are majesty and beauty, and we believe that majesty and beauty complement each other."

Now Dr. Ali changes the course of the conversation, "Who is the King of Humans and Jinn? For us it is Ali, Zain Al Abideen (son of Imam Hussein), who said when he left the field of Karbala, 'If everyone between East and West dies, I would not feel lonely because I have the Quran with me.' So we are tranquil and secure as long as we are with the Quran. So if you are serious, Kabir, you will roll up your sleeves and enter a contest with Barbara Cartland[5]. You must write a book that will sell to the whole country!

"But now we have to go back and memorize the quatrain!" he commands with a clap.

A healer through abundance (Kawthar), the one of the lights, heals me,
And Saleh through the seven binary opposites gives me to drink,
Allah is the Light and the Bestower. His smiles are like an olive,
the camel of the signs brings me to life.

شافٍ بكوثرَ ذو الانوار يشفيني
و صالحٌ بالمثاني السبع يسقيني
الله نورٌ و ذو فضلٍ
مباسِمُهُ زيتونةٍ ناقة الآياتِ تحييني

"We'll see today who memorizes this first, Kabir or you!" he says to me as he asks me to recite. "Fantastic! When we re-evaluate this

---

5. This is something of an "inside joke." Ms. Cartland is an author who has sold hundreds of thousands of romance novels, who Dr. Ali cites as an example of the popular interest in the subject of love, a subject to which he feels the Sufis have a superior claim.

quatrain we see how it has taken the juice of the four Surahs of today[6] because 'the seven binaries' are in *Hijr*, 'light' is in *Nur*, 'abundance' is *Kawthar*, and we will see how He pointed to *Abbasa* with 'His smiles.'

"The Ayat says Allah is the Light—what number is it? Thirty four, it's the 34th Ayat of Surah Nur. This is a very important number. It is the one after 33, meaning, it's the second life of the Messiah. Allah wants to bring light through music, because the dance of light, the vibration of light, is a movement of sound. It is a wave, they call light a wave. Observe! Count with me: 'God is the light of heavens and earth.' OK, let us make this clear. It is understood one way by the majority, but now explain to me more deeply: 'His light is as a niche within which is a lamp, the lamp is in a glass, the glass is like a jeweled star lit from a blessed tree, an olive not of East or West, its oil almost lights up though no fire touches it.' I will tell you! The resonances are 1–Do (the niche), 2–Re (the lamp), 3–Mi (the glass), 4–Fa (the star), 5–Sol (the tree), 6–La (the olive), 7–Si (the oil). These are the musical scales of light! Now the next Do is Light upon Light," he exclaims as he claps his hands together for emphasis.

"We'll see how He brought to existence the relationships that are equivalent to music. In Ayat 87 of Hijr we find *And verily We have brought you seven of the binaries and the tremendous Quran*. The Quran is the new DO. There are the seven binaries, and then the eighth is light upon light. The whole of the Quran is light upon light because the words are lights and lamps that take you to the greatest light! This is in Hijr. In Nur we see the seven similitudes of light and light upon light. Notice the correspondence of the seven in Hijr and the seven in Nur. The niche corresponds to the first binary."

"This is the new Do, it is still Do, Do, Dieu. *Light upon light* means that the relative ascends to reach the absolute. He has passed on to the new ladder to the new scale. *Light upon light*—that's 8.

---

6. This refers to a system of assigning to each day four surahs: one being the day in the Islamic calendar and its number equivalent among the Surahs; two being the Surah equivalent in the order of temporal revelation; three being the day in the Western calendar and its corresponding numbered Surah; four being the corresponding Surah in the temporal order of revelation.

Eight is beautiful because it begins the whole octave again! Are any of you jealous of eight? Do you want an explanation for eight? From now until a million light years later we will not get to the end of explaining eight! Light upon Light. God guides to His light whomever He wishes and God strikes similitudes for people. He explains to us for thousands of years His names and attributes and then He says: this is just a similitude! And God has knowledge of everything. This Allah, the Light," he concludes as his voice lowers as if in awe of the words. "Hence in *The Lights of the Qur'an*[7] this is the music, this is the sound of the lights. Have you ever heard anything like this?" he turns to ask and laughs, "It's a new wine and a new light, I mean it's a new music and a new music of light."

★ ★ ★

---

7. The three books translated here, which comprise *The Civilization of Paradise*, are taken from Dr. Ali's masterwork, *The Lights of the Quran*.

Addendum

Civilization of Paradise is the most complete translation of *The Lights of the Qur'an* so far. *Happiness without Death*, published in 1992, presented 30 poems corresponding to the first 30 Surahs revealed to the Prophet Muhammad, peace be upon him. *Civilization of Paradise* completes the cycle of poems corresponding to the 114 Surahs of the Qur'an, with five additional poems corresponding to the five times of Islamic worship.

Purity of the Way

*Translated by Ibrahim Shihabi, Kabir Helminski
and Camille Helminski*

Glorifications

Sūrah al-Qiyāmah (75)

You, Compassionate One,

have emerged from Your Autonomy
as revealing light.
In each fingerprint You publish
the record of our deeds.
You have revealed Yourself; and each soul
knows the Tenderness whose Source You are.
You orient humanity
toward its own well-being.
You have revealed Yourself
and the Life hereafter,
because You alone are the Bestower
of life and of death.
First You create life; later You restore it.
You bring us to completion.

Adversity matures us.
The cold is an adversary;
so we seek the heat of fire.
Hell is an adversary;
so we search for paradise.
The human mind is noble;
so we love the Best.
We practice a chemistry,
combining the elements by their primordial unity.
The prophets' laws, proportioned to humanity's needs,
Confirm the oneness of revelation.

You have revealed Your Self,
and Springs of yearning flow forth:

Water, sublime beings, perfect words.
Words, language, languages—guide me
to the forms of glorification that suit You best.
You are more than all praise and thanks.
You, the Absolute Compassion.

Aspirations

Sūrah al-Humazah (104)

You, Compassionate One,

have revealed Yourself: fidelity is a language,
because You are the aim of all aims.
All currencies circulate for Your sake;
in all times all issues are submitted to You.
You have revealed Yourself and love is a necessity,
because You are the All-Knowing.
Existence requires discovery
the discovery of forms and rules.
You have revealed Yourself; activity and creativity
emerge, for You alone sustain life.
All creatures' efforts are only
to support and clarify this.

Your qualities are gifts.
You bestow on Your creatures.
You teach them the best praise.
You are All-Hearing, full of mercy and lovingkindness.
You are All-Forgiving, Thankful, Creator of the heavens.
O Creator of Heavens and Earth,
the soul is purified by these words.
The mountains look up to You, Most Powerful.

You have revealed Yourself, so all languages,
all gifts, overwhelm our aspirations with satisfaction.
How holy are being, eloquence, and perpetuity.
By Your hand the heavens and the earth are folded
like the pages of a book,
because You are the most Compassionate.

The Ladder

Sūrah al-Mursalāt (77)

You, Compassionate One,

have revealed Yourself
on a scale from the actual to the ideal:

the reality of humankind and nature,
and all the kindness and splendor they include;

the gentle beauty of childhood;
the strength and glory of youth;

and the terrifying line of demarcation—
death, like autumn after spring.

The prophets, like successive winds
told us about their God in the form of religions;

and taught us how to think and work
through all the degrees of reality and idealism.

They drew our attention
to what is wrong and what is right.

To distinguish between them
conquests occurred.

Wise words were spoken
and treaties were made.

Alexander, Solomon, and religious communities
stirred things up with their conquests and their books.

Khayam, Epicureus, and Abu al-A'tahia,
Hafiz, Sadi, and Goethe
stir things up with words and poetry.

You have revealed Yourself,
and destiny is a rising path,
a staircase from the actual to the ideal.

The ship of prayer carried me
up the steps created
by the Maker of the lamps of the sky.

I ask You to make me pure
in the celebration of Your praises,
because You are the Absolute Compassion.

The Feast

Sūrah Qāf (50)

You, Compassionate One

The House has been decorated for the Feast[1]:
The ground is its carpet,
and the sky is its roof.
The sunlight-threads and the rain
are the Feast's decorations.
And all the world's springs and streams.
The sailing isles, as well,
are the Feast's ornaments.
The beautiful forests
are the crowds of the Feast's beauty.
God has inspired us,
so we worked and sang.

World friendships,
the discoveries of scientists, and
the auspicious signs of those who established religions
are all ornaments and marvels of the Feast.
Prayers in secret and in the open,
poets' writings, and
the ambitions of linguists
are all but the sweets of the Feast.

What is this world's Feast?
What is the meaning of the Universe's celebrations?
What is the mystery of renewal?
What is the mystery of the original seasons of creation?
Is it for anything but Your creative manifestation?

For You are the Absolute Compassion.

---

1. Al Eid

The Yearning

Sūrah al-Balad (90)

You, Compassionate One

Why am I filled with yearning,
travelling so many lands,
befriending all creatures,
bringing together the people of the word?
What is to be found
in the books of all times?
I gather the contents
inscribed in every age,
in all the verbal costumes
that language expresses.
What is this? And why?

I contract friendships daily;
friendly documents are exchanged,
agreements for trade, relationships,
relations of war and peace,
of peel and core, of East and West.
What is this? And why?

Should I swear I am in love,
a lover seeking love's satisfaction?
I swear by love,
and by love's God.
I swear, I swear,
I swear You are my God.
Bestow Your compassion
upon my heart,

for You are the Absolute Compassion.

The Protector

Sūrah aṭ-Ṭāriq (86)

You, Compassionate One

I observe how night sleeps;
and how the first light of dawn rises;
how the morning star appears,
and brings good news of victory.
With the laughter glistening in its eyes
like dew drops on the rose petal;
saying: "The sun is approaching;
awaken, people of the soul.
I am the star. Listen,
arise to meet the light of this day
and discover the happiness it contains."
This I observe. Why?

To see the star of piercing brightness at dawn,
to record the hymns of dawn,
to see the mystery within the mystery.
Isn't there some mystery behind the sun?
Isn't the sun mysteriously propelled?
I observe the luminous child of dawn,
and fashion poetry from its vocabulary,
and set it to the music of life.

Why does dawn awake me
with its child and her laughter?
I observe the child of dawn, listening . . .
I hear her telling me the secret
of the aim of all that is manifest.
All human souls are held
by their Protector,
because You are the Absolute Compassion.

The Moon

Sūrah al-Qamar (54)

You, Compassionate One.

The moon reveals the wonder of order.
What is this order?
I follow it during the month,
and each day a letter is taught.
The first is "alif;"
The second, "ba;"
the third, "tha."
and continuing, I pronounce the letters of the moon.
The moon sets
and I remain reflecting upon its return and its mystery.

I contemplate the list, letter by letter.
I consider grammar.
I consider morphology,
philology, and calligraphy.
I think of dictation and composition.
All these letters are children.
A sound in the depths
tells of an ocean of longing.

The sound says:
"Contemplate the secret of looking closely."
Look closely into the mirror of the universe,
comprehend the cosmic radar,
and the secret will be revealed
clearly . . . clearly,

Because You are the Absolute Compassion.

The Grantor
Sūrah Ṣād (38)

You, Compassionate One.

When memory moves me
I jump over words,
over distinctions,
over intentions;
I race with all the power of the wind,
and Spirit races with me;
I fly toward horizons;
I wander the fields of vision;
I circle, and return, and begin again
in a breeze, or in laughter,
in silence, in cries,
secretly and openly. Why?!

The Most Generous Assembly has divulged
the secret of a great message,
from before the beginning
until after the end.
You offer gardens.
You offer knowledge and strength
without limits.
You are the Bestower.

I am thirsty for the gifts of God Who manifests Himself.
I read the Message, the Qur'an.
So He guides me
within the possibility that is latent;
the memory, then, exists and offers life,
for You are the Absolute Compassion.

The Favor
Sūrah al-Aʿrāf (7)

You, Compassionate One,

have revealed Yourself and the eagerness of my heart
has opened universes;
has become infinite particles
in a dance of probability.
My eyeball, my eyeball,
has become a pen, become a pen;
sailing over words
like a vessel of yearning.

Longing guides it
to the meaning;
each letter lifts me up
to joy and gladness;
I wander through gardens;
letters of revelation
are ladders;
I go up, up,
until I reach the heights;
I know a secret;
I know a mystery,
neither the dialog of paradise,
nor the dialog of hell.

I recognize that this height relates to good deeds,
and that a height is the top of things.

So, from the heights I find a view;
the best way of being is to serve.
Allow me to know through Your highest quality
for You are the Absolute Compassion.

Training
Sūrah al-Jinn (72)

You, Compassionate One

have revealed Yourself, so my life is secure,
guarded by Your Message in every land.
Your soldiers have been trained by love
and by faith.
They may not be seen by anyone,
yet they may appear in anyone
astonished by meaning,
like the mystery and meaning in words.
I delight in the gardens
and the orchards of meaning that cover the land.
The trees of the orchard are languages,
and I wander through the worldwide garden.

I walk among the trees;
I talk with the beautiful breezes;
I transform the voices of desire
into the music of the wind.
I grasp the most powerful desires,
like the genie hidden in the throbs of the heart;
I train them until they are faithful,
and sing their prayers to the Compassionate One.

You have revealed Yourself, so my life is secure,
guarded by Your Message in every land.

What should I do, my God,
with all the countries,
to help humanity perceive that You are the First and the Last?
You are the Absolute Compassion.

Ambition

Sūrah Yā Sīn (36)

You, Compassionate One.

My ambition is greater than my words,
greater than all the languages of the globe,

greater than the paintings of artists,
greater than the world's music.
You, Compassionate One,
are an implied speech in my heart.
You issue orders through two letters,
the whole world, the entire universe.
What lies behind this world?
Who knows what lies behind it?
Have they known the mystery of the witnessed world,
and the laws of motion?

You, Compassionate One,
are an implied speech in my spirit.
It is explained by religions,
by science, by art.
Yet it is still new and novel.
I journey here and there hoping
that the awareness will direct me
to the source of this mystery.

May these words
fill the space of this world with effort,

and discover the source of meaning
and return with a sip of love's secret.

You may keep silent;
You may speak anywhere;
for You are the Absolute Compassion.

The Difference
Sūrah al-Furqān (25)

You, Compassionate One.

Your manifestation unifies with the Criterion[2].
The difference between Truth
and Falsehood
is like the difference between the core and the rind,
between the kernel and the chaff.

I unify by means of the Criterion,
that distinguishes people from behavior.

The people of the core and the kernel
have a house to gather in.

I'm heard by those who want to hear.
A dog's hunger does not equal a child's . . .
even an extremely loyal dog.
It's strange that a child dies of hunger
near the house of a well-fed dog.
Is there true love in that dog-owner's house?
What keeps the hungry child from being fed?

O God, Your manifestation unifies with the Criterion.
I distinguish the dog from the human being.
I keep the dog together with the dog
and the human with the human.

I ask Your mercy for all, for me,
from You, the Absolute Compassion.

---

2. Al Furqan

Nature
Sūrah al-Fāṭir (35)

You, Compassionate One,

who make my life easy.
You give me freedom.
Like nature I live through growing.
I train myself.
I gain experience
in this world.
I strive upwards
until I approach the Pure.
Then I say, "O, Creator
of my being,
how has this world
caused me to forget Your Supreme Nature?!"

Creator of my being,
I recall a wonderful dream.
I recall that . . .
What do I recall?
May I be allowed to remember?
O Creator of my being,
how sweet is the supreme dream,
and how easy it makes my life.
O Creator of my being.

What You give remains as You want it to be.
I recall a wonderful dream.
I recall that .. .
What do I recall?
I remember that
You've given me existence and life.
You, the Absolute Compassion.

The Virgin and Her Seclusion

Sūrah Maryam (19)

You, Compassionate One,

have filled my life with music.
Your love has carried me eastward on its waves.

Withdrawn into seclusion, the heart
saw Mary, the virgin, in her seclusion.
It saw her pure soul excited,
for God's words can present themselves as visions and ideas.

Your love is a sea that carried me on its waves westward,
and gave me the sweetest drink in the form of an ordeal.
People left me alone with my heart and tongue.
In my aloneness silence was prolonged.
Sounds became more and more subtle and sweet.
God's words are seen with the heart and tongue.

I prolonged this expansion with my own rhythm.
Your love is a sea of friendships.
Its waves carry me upon the truth.
I dive. I swim.
I see visions of music,
visions of innovation,
visions of religions and languages,
a sea with which love encircled me.

Your love has carried me on its waves
eastward and westward.

Am I a stranger in Your world?
You've filled my life with music.

My homeland is Your love.
My sea and my directions are Your love, as well.

You, the Absolute Compassion.

Reflecting
Sūrah Ṭā Hā (20)

You, Compassionate One,

have revealed Yourself.
My soul has become a tree
that yields fruitful ideas.
Languages and directions
are the branches of the soul.
Birds come from far away;
fishes comes as well.
From orbits,
from stars.
Shepherds come from the deserts;
fishermen come from the shores.
Our pastime is reflecting
on this arrangement.

We call You, the Absolute Compassion.
We call You by Your attributes.
We feel compassion
and we weep.
We call You, and implore You,
Master of the Throne, Compassionate One.
All that is on earth is Yours
and all that is in the Supreme Assembly.

Reflection is our pastime.
We openly honor Your creation.
In al the languages of the Earth's peoples.
Help this compassionate tree of Spirit.
You, Lord of the universe and of this tree.

The Garden
Sūrah al-Wāqiʿah (56)

You, Compassionate One,

have revealed Yourself, and so the garden has grown.
A spirit breeze lifts me.
I see paradise
and live in bliss.

The companions of the garden offer no empty words,
for their languages are music and peace.
This is a garden of golden divans,
drinks of energy and consciousness,
fruits of our choice,
the meat of birds,
and those beautiful, large,
lustrous eyes we love.

Hymns of prayer,
musical verses,
spirit of spirits,
garden breezes,
glorifications sung by water,
sung by fire,
sung by green, growing plants.

The music of paradise is sung with joy,
with the youthfulness of bodies,
with spirit's determination.
A spirit breeze lifts me up
to see paradise, to live in bliss,
for You are the Absolute Compassion.

Gilding

Sūrah ash-Shuᶜarāᶜ (26)

You, Compassionate One,

have revealed Yourself
and distinguished poetry from revelation;
and so, poetry has been distinguished from poetry.

I've known the command;
I've known the mystery.

For my home, I've chosen a high hill
overlooking the world
where the five rivers run.

Behind the rivers stretches
an ocean of secrets.

A sea of perfume,
of chaste hues,
perfume of the house
for the Lord of the House.
I mold it into various forms.
I shape it in various ways
like oil
that becomes light,
like ink
that becomes letters—
letters gilded
with the light of the eye.

With my letters I build joy
and rise, my chest filled with pleasure,

before the first morning light,
with the star preceding sunrise.
I offer myself in a letter of perfumed light
to You, the Absolute Compassion.

Warning

Sūrah an-Naml (27)

You, Compassionate One,

have revealed Yourself, and liberated the ants
from their reticence, and liberated the birds, as well.

One ant warns the others.
The hoopoe says, "I know what you do not."
To whom does it say this? To a chosen Prophet.

The story of Bilqis is well-known,
and Suleyman is the chosen prophet.

Like freedom,
like the All-powerful,
freedom, O my Sustainer, is happiness.
I meditate upon the themes of freedom,
and turn the millstone of mind.
I distribute the bread of reflection.
Each loaf speaks the warning of the ant,
and the cry of the hoopoe.
Why should bread be circumscribed?

To stir the thoughts of the one who eats it,
and to become like the ant in the valley;

to be like the hoopoe of Bilqis,
to inform a prophet,
and to draw the attention of his people
a statement is made:
You are the Absolute Compassion.

Fire

Sūrah al-Qaṣaṣ (28)

You, Compassionate One,

have revealed Yourself. My love was afire
in a snowy winter in a distant land.

Are the stories of my love
the stories of snow and fire?

Does this story have an end?

This year the snow was full of enthusiasm.
It covered the mountains,

embraced the trees,
settled upon rivers and springs,

and hid the roads and houses,
prolonging the time of inundation.

During that time
I was glowing with the fire of my love.
Its space was opening wide.
I used to go out and explore.
Attracted by that snow,
I went to the open country.
I said I must cool this burning,
but when I crossed the boundaries,

my fire found its pasture;
the snow melted.

Houses reappeared;
all those imprisoned were released;
warming fires danced everywhere.
And You are the Absolute Compassion.

Probability
Sūrah al-Isrāᶜ (17)

You, Compassionate One

have revealed Yourself. A carpet of wind lifted me, hovering.
I found the house[3] in every direction.

Prayers were possible
in all languages.

The language of clouds seeded in space.
The language of winds that carry the clouds.

The language of airborne iron.
The language of steering and of the pilot.

Motion drew no boundaries.
The heart rejoiced in worship's prostration.

What are these carpets in space?
What do I see?
Could this view be described?
No boundaries, no restrictions.
Does the plane carry me,
or do I carry it in my hovering?
My ecstasy is endless yearning,
ebbless expansion.

Science will always remain very insignificant;
what we know, very little.

For the greatest,

---

3. The Kaaba. The sanctuary in Mecca toward which all Muslims orient themselves in prayer.

the most abundant
is the specialization of another
being translated by Spirit
for all times,
and You are the Absolute Compassion.

The Bottom

Sūrah Yūnus (10)

You, Compassionate One,
have revealed Yourself.

The sea bottom attracted me.
How could I live at the bottom of the ocean?

Ninevah knows.
Jonah knows, and the whale knows, too.

Ninevah wasn't able to embrace its prophet.
It was narrower than the belly of the whale.

The whale's belly held Jonah,
and then heaved him safely onto land.

Like the one who thinks of a meaning
and then expresses it.

Why couldn't the prophet contain his people?
Jonah had to dive deep to the bottom,
and when he dove, he could see.
This vision saved his village,
an exception among villages.
And so, he deserved every praise.
Is there an ascent after dwelling at the bottom?
How precious are the treasures of the depths!!

To my village I return to teach about the ocean's expanse,
and to instill in them the heroism of the whale,
and instruct them in the anthem of salvation.
Faithfulness belongs to You alone, O Safety.

You are the Absolute Compassion.

The Flight
Sūrah Hūd (11)

You, Compassionate One.

A whisper moves me,
and so I soar into the space of history,

a fleet of ships unloading my cargo
upon continents,
explosives which erupt wherever they fall,
making lakes of dawn.

Al-Rub' Al-Khali in the desert
becomes rich with lakes.

The salt sea
empties the spoils of the two rivers out of its hand.

The explosive dawn
expands in the form of civilization.
Things change.
'Ad returns and kneels in worship.
After the explosion
came the decisive conclusion.
My body moves me.

I return with the whisper
to count those who remain alive,
and those who are born at dawn,
and all the profits of mankind
that can be measured.
You are the Absolute Compassion.

Dreams

Sūrah Yūsuf (12)

You, Compassionate One,
have revealed Youself.

My dreams are universes
and a spring season of colors.

Love entertained me
and negotiated with me for the people.

It remains,
knowing the secret of the supreme.
It negotiated with me on the matter.
I thought deeply.

Meanings come to me
as dreams, like a virgin spring.

The manifested dream has made me glow.
I heard the story of Joseph.
Its details: the purchase, the imprisonment;
then his escape
and reunion with his family,
embracing his brothers in love.
The strangest dream has come true.

I dream neither of love nor power,
but of another sort of universe.

My dream is the unfolding of color,
embracing the earth and all it contains,
so as to accompany the supreme rhythm.

You are the Absolute Compassion.

Unknown

Sūrah al-Ḥijr (15)

You, Compassionate One,
have revealed Yourself,

created times,
innovated creatures, and
educated humanity.

Music of wind,
music of water,
dance of fire
just after a wind has blown.

All joys are unified by a secret.
What secret?

I reflect on the matter.
I portray my key.
I break into the unknown,
open doors, view horizons, and
inhabit all kinds of happiness.
But a mystery
still remains behind all that is uncovered.

It will remain an unknown secret.
Even those with knowledge will not know it,
not even the contemporary men of knowledge.

Your mystery has its own key,
and first sign, O You who decide.

You, the Absolute Compassion.

Cases

Sūrah al-Anᶜām (6)

You, Compassionate One,
have revealed Yourself, and so my heart is adorned,
and joy has overwhelmed me

with faith embracing
and accompanying me;

groups of reciters
with visions of warning.

So I remain a companion to safety,
being assured

by everything's details
both in the morning and in the evening,
that You are the only One who gives,

who touches the dead with blessings,
and so blessed they return to life,
and by this touch
they flourish with life.

You are the All-powerful, the Good.
Your qualities are purely beneficent.
You are the All-powerful, the Good.
In Your pastures are the livestock.

My heart, adorned
with the love of Your manifestation,

chooses
whatever it likes.

You are Absolute Generosity.
You are Absolute Compassion.

Glow
Sūrah aṣ-Ṣaffāt (37)

You, Compassionate One,
have revealed Yourself, the active heart of the universe.

A rank of the faithful recites the Holy Qur'an;
another rank calculates the signs of God;
and yet another rank gives orders,
or prohibits, or orients
all sorts of creatures;
and, according to Your will,
sustains whatever is existent.

A rank clearly reveals,
and innovates the beneficence of worship.

You reveal Yourself.
The East and the West are Your servants.

Upon earth, in all orbits,
throughout the heavens,
between the Highest
and the Lowest.

You reveal Yourself, and my heart glows
as though I consciously stand in line
with those who recite,
or those who restrain;
or it becomes more transparent than languages and lives,
for You are the Absolute Compassion.

The Rhythm

Sūrah Luqmān (31)

You, Compassionate One,
have set the rhythym
from peak to trench.

The music of Your love varies.
It is a sail

I sail through the sea of the universe
the ship of my life

looking for my homeland
behind the rhythm.

The music of Your love varies.
It is a sail.

The laws of this universe
are echoes of the rhythm.

The words of God are
inexhaustable languages.

He is Dignity
and Wisdom.

Behind each sail
I sail in the universal sea.

The ship of my life
is looking for my homeleand
in the spirit of rhythm.

If the oceans were ink,
if the world's trees
were pens
of color . . .

You are the Absolute Compassion.

Life

Sūrah Sabāᶜ (34)

You, Compassionate One,

have revealed Yourself. My love has flowed like a spring,
running within my ribs,

opening the days of my springtime.

My day has its own criterion.
It may be an age or several epochs.

It may have flowers
and birds.

My springtime is a paradise
whose air is holiness.

My spirit glorifies God
accompanied by the spirit of paradise.

You have revealed Yourself.

Truth has come from the unseen.
Well-being has come, and subsistence, too.
Handsomeness and taste have come, as well.

The new soldiers
of a happy world
without borders.
I live in Your bliss.

You have revealed Yourself.

I am no longer afraid.
You have helped me, so my eye
now sees my heart's spring
and sings on every road:

You are the Absolute Compassion.

Generosity
Sūrah az-Zumar (39)

You, Compassionate One,
give generously in proportion to Your graciousness
and grant humanness.

I ask
covertly and overtly,

but I ask only of You,
Compassionate One.

I conceal my needs,
declaring none of them to people;

I conceal them from the jinn,
and even from myself.

All remain in the dark as regards my needs,
and even I, myself, O Compassionate One.

But I ask You,
the Absolute Compassion,
Your command is within my spirit,
a mystery that can't be exposed.
All the earth is within Your grasp.
And the heavenly universes are a book
I imagine I could . . .
Could I express myself openly? Could I ask?

Springs flow, stars glide
like meanings in the depths of letters.

Like a small book in a huge palm,
I imagine circling around
what I ask, but I do not ask.
You are the Absolute Compassion.

By Faithfulness
Sūrah Ghāfir (40)

You, Compassionate One,
grace me by guiding my way.
Through faithfulness I petition You.

I know that He, the Most High, teaches,

and creates the spirit by command,
and He, the Lord of the Throne, gives as He wills.

He decides the matter
by a slender movement
of graceful steps,
according to His creative command.

Only those granted being by You truly exist.
You, Compassionate One,
grace me by guiding my way
and say, "Call upon Me."
I call You, the Living One,
the only Sustainer.

O, God
help my heart to be faithful
and bestow honor on my life by glad tidings.

You, Compassionate One,
grace me by guiding my way.

You said, "Call upon Me."
I call You through the purity of the Way.
Command Your action by Your gifts,
You, the Absolute Compassion.

Genius of Spirit

*Translated by Mahmoud Mostafa
and Kabir Helminski*

The Sun is a Grandmother

Surah Fuṣṣilat (41)

My elements speak according to their nature,
so I ease into the dialogues of stillness.
This is the aspiration of poetry and poets.

Its music is the freedom of order;
it harmonizes its vast oceans with its hope,
as if hope were a spring
transforming minerals into pure love.

I came to love the secret conversation of the water and the dust.
The Spirit of the Water says to the Dust:
Do you understand the future?
The Spirit of the Dust says to the Water:
Whatever we accept together it is.

The Water: *Doesn't our mother have sisters?*
The Dust: *The daughters of the Sun are her sisters.*
The traveling planets are her daughters.

The Water: *Do our aunts have daughters?*
The Dust: *Let's suppose so, what is it that you want?*
The Water: *How do we talk if we meet?*
The Dust: *I put your hand in mine and we clap*
and the life of the seasons break into festivities.

And all who live upon the Earth flower with riches.
And there is no longer the shame of poverty for anyone on our planet.
Then we will invite our cousins to join us.
The Water: *And what is the situation with the daughters of the Earth,*
and with our grandmother, the Sun?

Maternal Aunt
Sūrah ash-Shūrā (42)

The elements in me
are consulting one another
in search of evidence of what is right.

I heard a human being at the earth's equator,
dry wind in his nostrils and hands.
arguing with the water and dust.

His argument was a consultation
through which the consultants
arrived at a human perspective,

For he is balanced in search of what is right.
My heart was in wonder
at the music of his dialect,
this one who rebels in childhood
and goes to excess in youth.
How did time bring him into balance?

And when did he admit my motherhood?
He said to his debaters and consultants:
we are earthly, this is our only nationality.

But our grandmother is the Sun and this has its meaning.
The children of the planets related to the Sun
long as much as we long.

Perhaps the children of Venus have more longing,
for I received a message from a UFO,
containing symbols that need to be grasped.

We need an expert and so we visit our Maternal Aunt.
So from all the treasures of our own Mother,
what gift shall we bring her?

Chiding

Sūrah Zukhruf (43)

At mid-day the sun sits equitably within my heart.
I feel the mother's relentless tenderness toward me,
purifying me
and burning away my pain.

My sons and daughters
don't like their grandmother at noon.
They prefer how she adorns them at sunrise
and what she displays for them at sunset.

My inhabitants like playing,
but my mother the Sun is serious, ever-renewing.
Though she plays with her grandchildren,
she disciplines them as well.

At the beach she gives them a golden hue
and singes them with her fire.
Then she spreads for them the bedding of night.

I feel that the Sun chides me
for being remiss,
since I am the mother responsible for those who rest in me.

Why do so few desire to cultivate me?
And why do I not attract all colors?
How helpless I am
when the human being
becomes complacent upon me.

Her rays wake them with the song of sunrise,
"Get up you lazy ones, get to work!
Even in the wilds, why neglect these virgin lands?"

Ocean of Smoke

Sūrah ad-Dukhān (44)

From You to You I am circling.
But sometimes the footprints of my people draw me in.
Then again You pull me away from their minute concerns.

And as You snatched me I experienced Your attracting.
I saw a vast smoke above a fire
and all of humanity falling into it.

O people, why do you swim in this ocean?
Ceaselessly, hours upon hours,
you swim then drown in the smoky Sea,
and again and again each day, giving yourself up to this.

It is a wonder that these bodies are re-invigorated for this.
The swimmer goes out a great distance
and yet is swallowed by the fathomless depths

I wait for him; wondering . . . when will he return?
And I scream with the loving agony of a mother:
O Lord! When will he return?

And earth is spread out in space . . .
enlivened by its human inhabitants.
Why do You overpower them with the smoke of the fire?
No one can escape from this . . . why then?

In my heart You whisper: O Mother of Humanity!
This is the fire of sleep and death.
Your children must awaken to be resurrected.

Maternal Aunts

Sūrah al-Jāthiyah (45)

I lie motionless between the hands of Your beautiful benevolence.
My heart never sways from Your love.
With Your blessed hands You feed me strength,
so how can I disobey You?

Obedience to You is the tree of life.
I seek its attractive shade,
and I endure through its fruits.

A traveler I am, among travelers.
As long as I can remember I've glanced at my sisters, wishing them
happiness.
They look at me and wonder,

"What is God's lowly Earth bragging about?
Is it her weak and conceited human beings?"
I turn toward another, more powerful journey;
the ship of the ascending human freely roams.

"Welcome," says the Moon.
"Peace," say the children of the Moon.
"Be secure," say other sisters.

As for the Sun, she sent the human being back to me
and said to him,
"Reconcile yourself with your earthly siblings, make things right
between brothers and sisters before you fly off to the houses
of your aunts!"

Acquaintance
Sūrah al-Aḥqāf (46)

One of my sons was angry.
In one hand he was carrying a basket of cauliflower,
and in the other he was carrying a basket of fruits and dates.
He had spent a long time gathering them,
and he was thinking they were good provisions.
Now for a while he would be relieved of search for sustenance.

Perhaps in this life he found a way to repel poverty.
But a beggar stopped him,
and pleaded with him to give him both baskets.
The first was for his sick mother.
The second was for his nursing wife.
The beggar said, "I saw you gathering them
and in the virgin wilderness I recognized your substance.
I liked your creative tenderness
so I followed you, seeking your company.
Then you attracted me more;
so I wished to strengthen the bond between us.
Therefore give me your provisions of cauliflower and fruit."

The one with the provisions presented them,
but he glared in the face of the beggar.
The beggar was embarrassed and left.
The other followed him hoping he would accept,
but the beggar did not turn around until he entered a faraway cave.
In the insightfulness of the cave
the one who had been asked came to know the one who asked;
and thus became joy.

Hero

Sūrah adh-Dhāriyāt (51)

I chose a champion from among my children,
a champion through whom I expressed my joy.
Just by saying this the earth is in glory.
A champion who renewed the spirit of history,
and walked alone in Truth, afraid of nothing but God.

O Lord! The mother discovers glory in the children of glory,
but, as You know, what glory does the earth,
rooted in this existence, offer?
The earth of this world is simple dust.
But Your subtle gift to the earth, O Lord,
grants her a son to be proud of.
This champion is an honor for this world.
He stands out like Truth; he fills us with hope.
He opens the paths to duty and responsibility,
and plants trees in the desert of liberty.

Rain clouds form lakes in the mountains of majesty.
A champion about whom I am happy to speak,
who is an honor to the world.
Through him knowledge comes to life and work blossoms.
O Lord! By the glory of Your light complete this light!
And with it make the power of Your love in him
extend through all civilization.

Two Wings
Sūrah al-Ghāshiyah (88)

There is nothing more beloved than You.
I say it in every language.
And nothing can substitute for You.
Let me reveal a little of Your constant beauty.

You brought me inside the forest canopy,
where springs are flowing, birds are singing,
and fruits are near at hand.
Winds of questioning played with my desires,
but You made the mountains of trust firm in me.

The lions of patience arose,
and the wilderness of complete reliance bloomed.
My wishes were powers without limit,
but the vision of You is so rich I forget everything else.

You clothed me with two wings, O God! What came over me?!
The wing of purpose carried me and did not fail,
and the wing of helplessness awakened my cry for help.
I sought mercy from You, enfolded in angelic dominion[4].

Then You carried me with two arms of eternal mercy
to the vision of You.
And what I cannot reveal happened.
There is nothing more beloved than You.
And nothing that can compensate for You.

---

4. *Jabarut*, a higher, creative level of spiritual reality.

Confidence
Sūrah al-Kahf (18)

I am the Earth . . .
I share with You my most intimate secrets
because You hold me in Your sight.
My confidence in this is absolute.

All those who intimately converse
have taken to my caves and my mountains.
I lay myself down for those who lean on me,
while I lean upon my confidence in seeing You.

You see me in such a way
that nothing can veil me from You,
You are the Concealer. You wrap me in Your night and day.

You shower my continents with the spray of the Sun,
and allow its inhabitants to pick the fruits of the day,
and You restrain the rain of light
so they may harvest the fruits of the night.

You see me and You lift the veils
for me to see the morning of Your Face.
I won't divulge the morning I see.
How could I express my joy!

I point to my overflowing capacity for happiness
and so I turn and turn forever.
You see me . . . You make me see a secret between You and me
that stirs the minds of poets to dream,
as do the scholars, and the gnostics, and the philosophers.

I become revealed,
and You become revealed

by all that they discover.
Your intimate promise is an eternal gift
by which I share my secrets with You.

The Loaf
Sūrah an-Naḥl (16)

I am the Earth.
I am placed like a loaf before the hungry.
Three hungry ones grab at my bread.
The armies and people of all three eat,
while the loaf remains a loaf and the hungry remain unfulfilled.
Every hungry one is a world of gluttony and power,
while the body of the Loaf is subtly resistant.

The hungry one from the East eats its hand,
and a new hand appears.
The hungry one from the West eats its leg,
and a new leg appears.
The third hungry one eats its head,
and it puts forth a new head.

Truly, the Loaf is the plaything of the hungry,
or it is rather the hungry that are the plaything of the Loaf.
If they are filled a bit they vie with one another.
Some tear the clothes of the others;
some wound the bodies of the others,
and then they all return to the marvelous body of the Loaf.
Did the spirit of reflection arise in their bodies?

The Loaf asks, "Who are you three?"
The first hungry one says, "I am the rich merchant."
The second one says, "I am the impoverished protestor."
And the third one says, "I am the visionary poet."
The Loaf says, "Where's the evidence for your claim?
One who is wealthy doesn't continue trading and competing.
The competitor is needy, while the wealthy one
is above competing.

He uses his wealth to meet the needs of those in need.
You are stuffed and yet hungry.
This is how you are.

And the protestor does not stay poor and complaining.
The complainer is weak, while the protestor
overcomes weakness and complaining.
He uses his sovereignty to wipe out poverty.
You are strong and yet afraid.
This is how you are.

The poet does not continue to imagine to foresee.
The one who imagines is deluded and bereft of his senses.
A poet feels his reality
and his essence and goes beyond both.
You are living and yet dead. This is how you are.
And you three are a brotherhood of hunger,
so take me and eat!"

The Inspired One
Sūrah Nūḥ (71)

I am the Earth.
I am witness to the striving
of the prophets among their people.

How adamant are humans
against their own well-being!
Their desires distort their essence.

Noah struggled long with his folk.
You know the story of Noah and his Ark.
What is the secret of disobeying Noah?

A prophet teaches a nation,
a man of firm will,
who lived close to a thousand years.

What secret is hidden in this failure in education?
Is it in the nature of his people
or in the method of his teaching?

He says: He went with them
along the paths of proclamation, making himself heard.
The story says: God answered his call.

So the prayer succeeded
though the call failed.
Thus was the deluge that destroyed the deniers.

Do you think civil war might be a deluge?
What good is intellect?
And what exuse do the intellectuals have?

Can they uncurl the tail of the dog?
In spite of this, teaching and teachers
remain a necessity.

The inspired leader always builds a ship
to save those who deserve
to inherit the earth.

Devotion
Sūrah Ibrāhīm (14)

I am the Earth.
I offered both my surface and depths to people,
so their resolve is suspended between depth and surface.

An ambitious one digs
in the depths for riches,
and a more modest one builds upon the surface.

People glide back and forth in the swing . . .
Whole civilizations are built upon the surface,
and still down deep secrets are hidden.

The built house is like the trunk of a tree.
Its inhabitants are its blossoming branches.
Who has thought about the roots below?

The grave is the root of the house.
And this is the freedom of the future.
Ya Rabb![5] People oscillate between my surface and my depth.

I found your people in both the house and the grave.
You know the revealing of my secret
and the depths beneath my surface.

I protect myself with Your majesty from the harm
of the whisperings upon my surface and in my depth.
You . . . Sustainer . . . Sovereign . . . Deity.

Humans and Jinn are surface and depth.
And my heart is a revolving circle whose concern is
You, O *Rabb*. Light up my path!

---

5. Sustainer, Nurturer, Lord.

So that the leader
will shine forth among my people
and protect the secret and the trust of my *Rabb*.

And so the galaxies will spin with the earth,
and You, Power of Creation, are praised by languages.

A Heart and a Fruit

Sūrah al-Anbiyāᶜ (21)

I am the Earth.

O Originator of the Heavens and the Earth!
You have freed me from the prison of doubt.
You have established me in the space of certainty.

You have taught me what to ask, for You are all I ask for.
You have taught me how to ask.
May Your gifts to me be in proportion to Your generosity.

Let me stand before You, through You,
so that the knowledge of all things will blossom in me.
While I arranged my works, it was You who fashioned them for me.

I have regulated the duration and extent of eating and sleeping,
and I have contemplated what was and what is yet to be.
My breast is both pillow and meadow.

The buds of the roses are the blush of a miracle.
You made me witness the spreading of the spathes.
You made me witness the discoveries of humankind.

The hopes of the water and the dreams of the dust,
the truth of Life in nature and humanity.
I opened the heart of a hopeful fruit, and found a seed embracing a bud.

I confided my secret to the bud
and it bloomed into a tall building.
I entered it and was greeted by a human lifespan.

It gave me the secret of a message:
Help the people enter the embassy of the prophets.

There Is No Name for Me

Sūrah al-Muᶜminūn (23)

I forgot my own name,
but Your name attracted me.

I succumbed to the pull of two wings,\.
Your favor and Your forgiveness;
through them I move and turn.

With the wing of Your forgiveness
I transcended the continents of the world.
With the wing of Your favor
I transcended the continents of action.

O God! How amazing it is to transcend!
The extent of selfish greed and arrogant heedlessness
seem like the landscape of an ant!

How could I restrain my actions
with the two wings of an ant?
Yet with the two wings of Your attraction I soar.

What are these vast galaxies?
I worship You, turning as they do,
and that is my remembrance.

In this vastness I find rest with You
and that is my empowerment.

Speech and silence are both powerless here.
Vessels of knowledge, action, and sincerity
float in the orbit of patience.

I have faith in You; there is no name for me.
I surrendered to You and found safety.
For You I am just as You choose me to be.

The Hero to be Sung
Sūrah as-Sajdah (32)

In my breast, O Lord of the Earth, are contradictions:
A child glides playfully in a swing
and next to him men are hanging in nooses.
One swings . . . one hangs;
and they are one human in my breast!

And I am the mother who is spread out under their feet.
Whom should I love more, the one who's playing in the swing?
Whom should I love more, the hanged man or woman?

Throughout the ages many of my children have gone astray,
and You sent the messengers and the prophets to them.
The prophets made it known they came to guide.
Does a prophet serve one who is lost?
This is a matter for contemplation.
Should I love the executed sons,
I who am the mother of the earthly children?

I prostrate myself. My face submits to the will of my Rabb.
I gather the different kinds of creatures into unity.
All dwellers should have the right to dwell peacefully.

Forms . . . forms appear in the inhabited places.
Forms . . . forms come from my deserted spaces.

Who knows? The woman rejected,
deserted upon the earth.
She may be the one who bears the hero to be sung.

Blending

Sūrah aṭ-Ṭūr (52)

My mountains glorify discovery.
I dive in the depths
to the summit of one of these mountains.

On the way to the summit
I saw horizons inside the tunnel.

I plucked a walnut and its bird flew far.
It carried me in the ship of its wings
and landed me upon the peak of Mount Sinai.

The light was like a cloak embracing the road.
I thought about the mountain's perseverance
before the birds of lightning,

So the depth of the sea shone brightly
upon the top of that mountain,
and the fish and birds mingled in the pool—fins and wings.

The image was apprehended,
but the struggle with the self was severe,
and so I freed myself of it.

I, truly, am not the Earth, nor my inhabitants.
The dust of every resentment is swept away.
Stillness submitted and silence prostrated,

then I saw You in everything and beyond everything.
Resurrection is through You and You are the Self–Subsistent.
You alone, You alone are the meaning,
both in withholding and bestowing.

An Eagle and Single Purpose

Sūrah al-Mulk (67)

I am the Earth.
To You belongs the Dominion,
O You, who are the originator of the heavens and earth.

I try to ascend through my efforts,
yet every tree and bird sings:
You are truly the unique one; there is no one like You.

And the light of gnosis and the word of knowledge repeat:
There is no one like You;
You who are alone in sovereignty.

Your scale is life and death,
in which You weigh all deeds and probe creation:

Whoever made his words the abode of his knowledge,
and whoever made his heart the dwelling of his gnosis.

O God! Make my heart Your restful home,
and let those who dwell in You be the tranquility of my spirit,
and make stillness the transformer of my self.

So it will be secure and traverse the universe
upon the eagle of knowledge.
And make me of only one purpose, O God,
and let it be You!

From You

Sūrah al-Ḥāqqah (69)

I am the Earth.
The gardens summon me like a mother,
and I attend the opening of the green and the yellow.

The gardens celebrate the feast of green,
whenever a tree becomes verdant.
Whenever a bush becomes verdant,
nature fills my hearing with shouting.

The gardens are sad in the funeral of the yellow.
Whenever a grape leaf turns yellow,
whenever a rose petal falls,
Nature fills my hearing with an uproar.

I neither celebrate nor mourn.
Truly, the greening of one leaf signifies all greening
and the yellowing of one leaf signifies all yellowing.
A yellow or green leaf does not warrant all this shouting.

Gnosis and circumstances are all in the leaf.
It has enslaved people in sadness and happiness.
I have removed my relationship to gnosis,
and I have flung off my causes that are tied to circumstances.

I connect myself to You.
I persist for You.
I ask of You,
and You are sufficient for me.

My Languages

Sūrah al-Maʿārij (70)

The ascent to Your presence is not long,
for You are a sustaining presence.
What is long is the sincere separation from what is other than
You—
the attractions standing along the path.

There is not just one sacred struggle,
but two: a lesser and a greater one.
With the lesser one armies and arsenals are resisted.
With the greater one the self-ness of selves is resisted.

I struggle with the two small ones,
and I struggle with the two great ones.
I triumphed in my homeland and my people,
I triumphed in my learning and my work.

I seek from You succor in my heart,
I ask of You purity in my freedom.

I thank You, God, for You have made me ascend.
I have no heart . . . but I have a Sustainer.
I am free from the attractions.
Your face is for me . . . only You I see.

I speak all languages,
and the translations all have one meaning.
You are the meaning.
All my languages are about You.

Virgin

Sūrah an-Nabāᶜ (78)

I am the Earth.
My dust awakens its senses to perceive the path of knowledge
and to journey toward knowing.

The path is an interconnected net invoking Him,
like the net of a fisherman calling the holy virgin of the sea.
The threads of the net are schemes of temptations.
O virgin, come to me . . . Do you recognize me?

Discover my face in work, in memories, and in thought.
Discover my hand in planning, in learning, and in understanding.
Discover my body in realization, in acts of remembering,
in acts of seeing, and in acts of peering out.

Discover my love in what is unchanging,
in what is familiar, and in what is different.
Discover, discover, O Beloved of Time.

My life: I am the virgin supported firmly.
I stand before Him.
He raised me up through seven clear stages.

The renewal of the path, and the celebration of the truth,
and the rivers of determination,
in the paradise of attaining I completed the overture,
the finale, and the place of rest.
So the music was complete.

This is my news. I am the Straight Path to Him.
Come, you envoys, let us describe Him.
For this is the way of realization.

The Guide
Sūrah an-Nāziʿāt (79)

I am the Earth.

The tranquility of my farthest reaches is the greening of hope.
No teller can adequately tell of this awesome greening.
I live the transformation of greenness, hue by hue.

The prophets came with clear signs.
The champions and righteous have struggled.
In the Garden are the righteous;
in the Fire are the corruptors.

The lightning flashed and receded,
carrying with it the account of those who have perished.
What carries those who are coming?
Power in war and peace, and love in ignorance and knowledge.

The powerful and the lovers eat,
and then are enfolded in the grave.
They resurrect awakened, and the Guide appears
to erase all poverty and oppression.

The earth is implanted with abundance; justice reigns.
All manifestations indicate and tell, I am the Earth.
I know what they embellish and beautify.
I reside in Your love above what they manifest.

Exalted are You, O Lord above the conjecture of languages,
and above whatever they ascribe.

A Sparrow

Sūrah al-Infiṭār (82)

I am the Earth.

I see You in every beating heart You sustain.
Through You I seek You
and guide others towards You.

In the heart of a wet sparrow
I saw Your exceeding mercy.
It swam with the longing of life
and with water You cooled the heat of its fire.

I saw its feathers made golden by the sun,
and how the breeze and the silence
made it dance in the shade,
as if under heaven is the meeting of the farthest extremes:
the sun, the air, the fire, and the water
and this music spreading song.
I listened to the spring sending forth the seas and poetry.
I heard a tender longing fluttering in the scent.

How did God unite us after we were both far away?
He arranges destinies with a vast and wise ability,
merciful and forgiving. It lifts us
high with spiritual intensity and
experiential taste.

I rose up, O Lord, to seek through You
the glory of Your everlasting bounty for this sparrow.

Birthing
Sūrah al-Inshiqāq (84)

I am the Earth.

My letters emerge from contentment split open,
and with contentment I split open my breast
so gardens will grow.

Fragrance, melody, and nourishment gather in these gardens.
What compelling beauty sings here,
its lips like virgin fruits?

The tree trunks pull in the wind,
a wind that is the voice of many hearts.
Gladness fills me,

Whenever seekers travel through my lands.
Whenever they bring forth my plants
and my daughters, I abide and go nowhere.

By Your awesome power
letters are born from letters.
Pine seeds birth a forest,
and smiles turn into children.

You hide secrets from Your own sight through Yourself
and through Your tender sight
You conceal secrets from Yourself.

This is why You are the able one, the concealer.
I love You, but I won't divulge how.
I stand steadfastly for You like the letter Alif
and I manage the wilderness.

So make me firm through You,
with firm words and deeds,
O Able One!

An Only One and a Woman of Sincerity
Sūrah ar-Rūm (30)

I admire my practical sons,
and my intelligent, skillful daughters.
There are great stories in the news.
They say the wise healers of the world
have accomplished the miraculous in medicine
and that people can now live in health.

The elixir of medicine has banished fear.
Among the listeners was a saintly woman
and her only son, in whom she invested a lifetime.
All the doctors in all their clinics were consulted.

She took him to every institution.
She cried out to them,
"What can you do, oh people of medicine?"
The saint's only child died.

She knew that the Sufficient One is not like all the created ones.
So she cried aloud with a tearful eye to the Truth,
"You are enough, and You are the Sustainer.
The great ones of the world are on the way like me.
They labor with difficulty upon all these paths
so that You may grant them the robe of intimacy."

Your Judgment
Sūrah al-ᶜAnkabūt (29)

The expressions of the poets make me laugh.
So do the discoveries of scientists.
They are like spiders spinning webs from saliva,
in order to trap their sustenance.
This is not a truly higher existence!
They've made exaggerated descriptions of You
and then took what they said for guidance.

If You wish for renewal they oppose whatever is new with You.
They try to show that renewal is wrong
by making analogies that they themselves made up.
But You are the Maker.
You skillfully master the most valuable truth,
and through the essence of mastery You renew every thing.

The desert turns into gardens,
an ignorant one learns, a little one grows to be a giant.
Is this new?
In Your hands is the Preserved Tablet,
and You are no accountant erasing and recording;
You are the Sustainer. Unique!
I accept only Your judgment in my heart.

The Mother

Sūrah al-Muṭaffifīn (83)

I am the Earth.
I plant Your love in my heart's secret.
I protect it from scarcity and exposure.
I sprinkle it with the verdure of my letters,
and water it from the blood of my spirit.

The blood of the spirit is a pure river from Paradise
in which swim virgins and pure-eyed ones,
from blood cells, white and red.
Your secret rises up in the sheathes and becomes the bread.
Then the hungry ones eat it,
and it becomes strength for body and soul.

The secret manifests in the beauty of a face,
in the wisdom of an intellect and tongue.
The lovers love it;
they write songs of confessions to it.
They glorify it, but they know not whom they glorify.

The geniuses of spirit are not heedless.
They praise You whenever a loaf upon a table smiles,
whenever an eye revels in a face.
You bring joyful companionship in all loaves and all faces,
the way You bring the joyful companionship
of a regal repast to the hunger of the one who fasts.

Foster Brotherhood

Sūrah al-Baqarah (2)

I am the Earth.
I revolve with energized tranquility.
The force of velocity sets me on fire,
but You pull me toward surrender and I rush to You.

I follow the Creative One and I am safe from distortion.
I bring forth my tender green grass
so a nursing cow will graze and be full of strength,
and so her udder will be full of milk.

The child of woman drinks whatever the calf does not.
Their two offspring grow together;
both are my children from the grass,
but I sacrifice one for the other.

The son of the cow serves the planting of the son of the woman.
Then the son of the woman slaughters his grass brother
and eats the flesh of his foster sibling.
Both of them were nourished by the milk of the cow
because she was endowed with strength and submission.

The defeated ones pretend to weep over the son of the cow.
For in their blood the milk of the cow
has overcome the milk of the mother.
But the wisdom of the cow is deeper and more powerful;
the milk of the cow and its flesh aspire
to be transformed to humanness.

So why do the weepers turn toward what is bovine?
The cow is a power longing to unite with the mother's milk,
so that it may become a sustenance
that ascends in the power of humans.

I am the Earth, I repeat my turning.
I renew my grass to fatten the cows and to sate the humans.
I love both the grass grazers and the milk drinkers.
I declare this love to all nations
so that equality will be in Nature.
Cows do not eat human flesh.
Justice is in heeding Nature.

I turn to implement Your just will.
My submission to the cycle of the seasons
is my safety and immortality.
Through Your name my grass dances in the pastures.
Through Your name the grass-eaters are slaughtered
so that they may become the sustenance and strength
of their foster brothers of the grass.

The Essence of Man
Sūrah al-Anfāl (8)

I am the Earth.
You expanded me in space,
and You mingle me with whatever You wish.
My valleys become verdant through praise.
The seasons of my valleys, pastures, and fields
are firm hands to gather the harvests.
They are resolute, renewing agriculture,
by all these good intentions and unflagging ambitions,
devising curricula for advancement and ascendance.

It may be that my soil softly enfolds,
and the compliant weakness in my religion is made pleasing.
So for what is all this striving of yours?
For whom are you gathering the seasons and the spoils?

Shall I tell the softness of the soil about the strength of religion?
Shall I announce to whom the gifts belong?
I reflect about punishing the muddy, obstructing earth.
No—rather, I think about strengthening it.
This mixture of water and dust,
must this bring weakness and flaccidness?
Why can't this mixture offer a third possibility?
You revealed to me a teaching for the clay
and I taught it how to comply and bring forth life,
and I prepared it to become the matrix of the roots,
and I established my agriculture upon the softness of the soil.
So the strength of abundant seasons blossomed.

When the whisper of Your guidance touched the soil,
bread came from the ears of its wheat,
perfume came from the lips of its roses,

150

honey came from the openings of its flowers,
and shade came from the tenderness of its trees.

These spoils are gifts and bestowals,
some harvested from military victory,
but for whom is the harvesting of gifts in war?
And for whom is the harvesting of gifts in peace?
Are they not for the teacher of the clay
so the clay may become fertile and supportive?
You inspired me to look around,
so I gathered in unity all the directions of my eyes towards You,
and You made me witness the gem-like essence of man
for whose sake You made me fertile.

Pure Discernment

Sūrah Āl ʿImrān (3)

I am the Earth.
I make room in my breast for every member of the family.
Those who have the color of thirst
drink from the springs of my breast.

My children, black and white, at the family feast,
are all fed with the bread of friendship.

My continents are expanses of air,
equitably, for those with nostrils;
and expanses of water, equitably, for those with gills.

I love both the fish and the birds.
Love's equity is in differentiation.
If I do not differentiate between the sparrow and the trout,
I would kill the one with water and the other with air.
I would be a murdering mother in the name of justice.

Equality is harmful when it does not see clearly.
So choice is justice.
A genius is chosen to help his normal brothers,

and so the prophets and the revolutionaries are chosen,
and thus night and day are differentiated.

The members of the family are like the organs of the body;
my heart sends nourishment to the eyes, ears, and hands.
This is equality, merciful and just.
I assign the eye to observe the sights,
and I assign the ear to translate the sounds.
The equation is clear in our extremities and our senses,
and so it is with just differentiation among people.

Simultaneously I equate and differentiate.
This is justice within the family.
I choose an honest leader for a country,
one who knows the secret of familial affection.
He rises to the responsibility,
offering both morsels and morals for his family.
The life of values is his poetic sensibility,
and his throne is his faith in the Divine
and his confidence in mankind.

I choose him as a protector of the dust and the young,
to serve justice in the human family,
to judge with equity and discernment at the same time.
They are the two sides of the scale.
Through balance God and humanity are content together.
I am the Earth, Mother of Contentment.
Patiently I protect truth and responsibility.
So grant me the wisdom of truth and patience,
O Sustainer of the sunrises and sunsets.

Harmony
Surah Al Ahzāb (33)

I am the Earth.
It gladdens me that You are the Exalted.
To You belong Displeasure and Contentment.
I seek refuge through Your everlasting exaltedness
and my heart rests in this secure sanctuary.

I see no other but You and I pull everyone else with me.
I shape the moments of time into groups.
In the group of Spring the creatures
are agreeable to one another in heart and action.

The group resonance is liveliness and vitality.
All who are related to Spring strive
for the sake of the vitality of the world.
How can the world live happily? Through harmony.

How do we harmonize each different race and nationality?
Whisper: *Beyond displeasure and contentment*
A pure spring flows from Eternity.
Time is a unity that branches like a tree.

The gathering of Spring,
and the gatherings of Summer, Autumn, and Winter
are the forms and practices of liveliness unified by time.

The true Human grasps the secret of oneness;
and knows that intelligence and mastery
are the partisans of the Time.

I, The Human Being

*Translated by Kabir Helminski
and Ibrahim Shihabi*

The Light of Satisfaction

Sūrah al-Mumtaḥanah (60)

I am the human being.
Mountain peaks rise far into space.
My sons' horses have wings of heavenly yearning.
My daughters' rooms are dreams of light.
I intended to move at dawn on Wednesday.

They talk about the Phoenix, a legendary bird,
that passes by during one of hope's many nights.
Its feathers are cities that grant wishes to people,
and he who sees it will be eternal.

Our road is full with ports of call and night journeys;
the eyes turn the pages of the sea book wave by wave,
searching the sky's galaxies star by star;
observing the crossroads, road by road,
sons and daughters have become active.

Each heir examines his or her possible ambition;
each heir wants to meet the Phoenix.

While I was passing through my experiment,
I wandered among seven sentinels:
the red one is in charge of fire, roses, wheat, and azarole;
the orange one glows in the orange plantations, farms, and in sunset;
the yellow one trains the genista flowers and the moon bowls;
the green one pitches its tents in the forests of cedars and oaks;
the blue one seeks livelihood in the depths of heavens and seas;
the Nile green hides the desired treasures for those who look for them;
the violet camouflages virgin canals for the soul's ships.

The myths of the seven guards have charmed me,
so I slept while awake and observed the colors,

157

and when the Phoenix landed on my head,
all the colors and shapes disappeared,
and the light of satisfaction embraced me with no barrier.

By Virtue of You

Sūrah an-Nisā^c (4)

I, the human being,
can achieve my salvation and sincere devotion
by virtue of You, not by myself.
Groups of female human beings form crowds;
they are commanded by womanhood
and forget the roots of language in life.
She's a woman whose root is motherhood.
When will she regain her origin?
When will the branch give its original fruit?

My salvation and sincere devotion can be achieved only
by virtue of You, not by myself.

Things reconceived throng all around me:
Gold, reconceived, becomes the veneer of banknotes.
Cheap wood re-varnished is treasured.
Man's worthiness is so diverted by his compulsions
that the assassination of sons by fathers is called "Victory,"
and the assassination of fathers by sons is called the "New Order."

My salvation and sincere devotion can be achieved
only by virtue of You, not by myself.

The crowds of galaxies encompass me,
and oceans of blood surge in my heart;
You, O my Creator, turn over their waves,
in sound and in silence,

In response and in restraint.
The mystery of such turning over has only one meaning;
only one meaning: You, O God, O God.

My salvation and sincere devotion can be achieved
only by virtue of You, not by myself;

I repent and invent, for I repeat an eternal truth.
Please, help my repetition, I, the human being.

The Power of Perception
Sūrah az-Zalzalah (99)

I am the human being.
Aren't You the donor of power and knowledge?

You've granted me the mountaintop,
and taught me the art of building;

Rocks are like untamed fillies;
I've mastered the art of breaking horses,
and tamed the rocks of the summit;

I dug a lake as wide as imagination
and received the weeping clouds as guests;
the clouds filled the lake with their joyous tears;
the sky would be happy if I invited its daughters, the clouds.

I made the sky happy
and purified the tears and adorned them with fish;
during the ages of light, I grew forests around the lake.

Champions of mountain climbing came to that place;
so did the geniuses of all nations.
They didn't go back,
because the summits, the lakes, and the forests can't be abandoned.

At the summit I stayed awake every night,
as if waiting for the Night of Power.

Please, grant me the power of perception and its blisses,
O my Lord!
Marvelous are Your decrees and revelation,
You've inspired the Earth to dance.

The earthquake took place upon Your order.
The water of the lake was distributed through the fallow land,
and to the trees of the summit, as well, and to the talented.

After the earthquake, I found myself alone.
Then You snatched me out of my loneliness,
and I saw my lake of the world.
I found myself dedicated to You alone,
and the dawn broke.

The Intimacy of Your Face
Sūrah al-Ḥadīd (57)

I am the human being.
The exaltedness of Your face is becoming my familiar atmosphere.
With a firebrand I lit a letter of mine.
I wandered inside the alphabet carrying that burning letter
and my alphabet caught fire,
and glowed like a sky adorned with stars.

A little from You is so much. Imagine receiving Your abundance!
I entered the burning forest of letters.
I distributed the torches among passersby,
knowing the results beforehand:

After some moments that equal thousands of years,
this progeny will overwhelm the forests of alphabets
and establish themselves as languages and dialects.

Festivals of tongues of fire will be held
and out of this iron will be forged.
Smiles of fire will fly with force
and the flying sparks will sprinkle the world with light.
Coveys of sparks, like flocks of eagles,
will flutter on the horizons of the wide globe.

I'll condense the light's brightness
and iron will, as a result, be tempered.
I'll make the mountains of iron transparent
and the intimate light will, as a result, be concentrated.

Yet, beyond letters and iron,
more dear than iron and letters,
more dear than joys and the of whole existence,
I wish for Your face's exaltedness as my familiar atmosphere,
I, the human being.

My Inheriting Children

Sūrah Muḥammad (47)

I, the human being,
stand among the nations of descendents,
and build civilizations on the lake of activity.

From his luxurious swimming pool,
one inhabitant sent greetings,
and a drunkard sent justifications:
I seize the pleasures of this day before tomorrow brings death.

A traveler waved saying:
I'm sailing along in the boat of rain.

An adventurous cavalier cried:
I've triumphed over the nations that I love.

Each heir plays a certain role.
How, then, could I deny any of these actors?
All of them are my inheriting children;
I give my ear to them all.

All of them kneel for the sake of their needs,
but I kneel only to You, O God.

That's the aim of my knowledge.
The wings of an eagle lifted me,
and I saw the wide sea
and glorified Your supreme attribute.

You taught me how to swim
so that I'll never drown, or be afraid or sad,
for You are the protector of mankind,
because mankind is a human being.

Liberated from Particulars

Sūrah ar-Raᶜd (13)

I, the human being,
have befriended the seasons' directions.

From one direction, I saw the prophets fighting for Allah.
From another direction, I saw the revolutionaries struggling.
From a third direction, I saw men of knowledge contemplating.
From a fourth direction, I saw nature expressing herself in her own way.

Love of directions attracted me,
so, I sought to understand:
Why does a scientist invent bullets that kill?
Why does nature make snow and burning heat?

I liberated the totality of my soul from its particulars
so flocks of birds flew out from inside it;
I flew by the power of my birds,
which took me high up in a three-dimensional ascent,

one of whose dimensions is a man worshipping the Creator;
the second dimension is a man talking to Him;
the third is a man sitting with Him.
I was astonished by the scene, and yet simply witnessed.
Then I woke up free from slumber and death.

I lowered my head, and contemplation
led me high over these and other worlds.
I did not stare around me, and so I was accepted among them.

Lightning winked at me;
thunder banged its drums.

I understood that they were glorifying the Creator,
but I didn't turn my eyes towards them,
so as to prove that the human is worthy of trust.

The Spring of Blood

Sūrah ar-Raḥmān (55)

I am the human being.
My memories play joyfully in the field of my inheritance,
asking for freedom and rejoicing exuberance.

Flocks of memories stray far and wide,
and I call the shepherd to gather them together;
but it's impossible for he has run after a tribe of bees
that hatched swarms in a mountainous cave
where he discovered a pure spring of blood.

Who has ever heard of a spring of blood?
Where does such a spring have its mouth?

It seems to be a small pond,
but, in reality, it is a channel to the whole ocean.
Its pours forth from all rejuvenated human beings.

I searched in the rocky open lands of history.
I thought it had another name.
So, I was attracted by a mysterious ardor to know it.
Its source has been discovered in millions of years.
It flows out of the Most Merciful; it is the Womb.
I joined my rivers with the spring of the Merciful's blood,
I, the human being.

On Intimate Terms with Things
Sūrah al-Insān (76)

I, the human being,
Confess to my love
for I am the lover on all the paths.

Poetry is a ray of my love:
a taste that seeped into the world.
It tasted the world's beauty and began to sing of these tastes.

Philosophy is a ray of my love:
a sort of logic that seeped into the mind.
It logically discussed relationships,
and revealed the methodology of cause and effect.

Science is a ray of my love:
it came to my hands and experiments began.

This experiment has ascended the tower of practice
and consequently civilizations have emerged.

I'm a lover, and I confess to my love;
I searched for the sources,
and selected whatever I wanted of metals,
throughout millions of years.

I cultivated the soil, so it has been glorified
and was sanctified and harmonious.
I opened the heart, so it kneeled, yielded to God, and made a sigh.

I have witnessed from high above motherhood and progeny.
From the mount of manifestation, the veils were removed.

I put on a veil of love's light, and penetrated the walls of existence;
I begot the virgins of knowledge,
so, months and letters were known through me.

I became intimate with things, so they revealed their secrets,
I became friendly with faces,
and so eyes came to be on intimate terms with me.
I became intimate with light and fire,
So they called me to recognition and friendship.
How then could I deny my love?
And how do I refuse to be my God's servant?
I, the human being.

Freedom
Sūrah aṭ-Ṭalāq (65)

I, the human being, confess my love of freedom.
I have been striving to liberate myself for millions of years,
but millions of restrictions direct me.

O God! What direction is this!
Would You let my soul lead itself by itself?

I stood at the door of the city
and the winds blew me away.
Rain and hail fell heavily and I was hungry.
The sun disappeared and my soul was depressed.
Tongues of countless needs called You.

A knight emerged glowing,
and the door of the city was opened.

I entered a world of richness and bliss,
and I followed the ways of the glowing knight.
He opened the door and guided me to happiness.
The ways of happiness are inventiveness, morals, and focus.
I direct my generations to these ways.

My heart has been opened and nourished,
and my soul has set out freely.
It invented an invention that recreates itself.

Among His creatures,
God selects those whom He wants to serve Him.
These chosen creatures manage matters with faith and knowledge.

I liberated my soul for light and water,

and for what they may disclose.
I divorced myself from all the restrictions upon my freedom,
And by means of freedom I confess my love,
I, the human being.

Without Memory
Sūrah al-Bayyinah (98)

I am the human being.
My memory exists in people and libraries.
Do You accept me with this memory?
How can I go to You with no memory,
no knowledge, no family, and no wealth?

One of my daughters needs me for a while.
She'll be very happy if I share a great joy with her.
What's this great joy? A lily that opened in the night.
She's learned a new word of a language,
or a handsome young man has come to ask her hand.

One of my sons needs me for a while.
He'll be very happy if I share the great joy with him.
What's this great joy?
The teacher at the elementary school praised him.
A young lady thanked him at a bakery
and restored the ground after one thousand years.

One of my sons needs me for a while.
He'll be very happy to be in my service.
What's meant by "to be in my service"?
To let him do whatever he likes with all that I possess;
to give him power and mastery over his brothers and sisters;
to dissolve my existence and let him take my place.

One of my daughters needs me for a while
to share with me her joy with a new dress;
or to participate in the discovery of a romantic poem,
in the discovery of a philosopher who engenders enthusiasm,
in the discovery of a hero who can defend and attack well.

My children ask for me on millions of occasions.

In millions of years, the memory of moments has been made.
How could You rid me of my memory?
Grant me a while, and I'll give You all that I don't know and do know,
and clear myself toward You, I, the human being.

The Colors of Eternal Power
Sūrah al-Ḥashr (59)

I, the human being,
explain to You what You know more than I do.
Your love leaks out from my words,
because of my trust in You,
as the musk bees fly in gardens,
their chests swelling with pleasure.

Being astonished by Your deeds,
I squeeze my probabilities until nothing remains but You.

Every time I give up myself, You give me hope and strength,
and renew me by means of the daylight and the darkness of night.

You give my life the colors of eternal power,
and so, I give up the seasons of my life for You.

And You give me power over the fields of death,
harmonizing between the fruits of wakefulness and dream.

Flocks of birds fly over my fields,
sowing them with the seeds of warblers.

I don't fear the treachery of sunrise,
but I have trust in the luxury of true transactions.

I only remember
the truthfulness of the breeze, the dawn, and the birds.

The creatures of the joyful garden will never be hypocritical;
they only bestow a glow upon me.

So, I glow with compassion
and go to You.
I joyfully do exercises of worship.
Thereby, the athletics of prayer link me with God's orchards.

In Paradise I reap the fruit of ecstasy
and construct the epic while I'm at the height of my ecstasy.

Shall I explain the epic of history
to the peoples of the day of Congregation?

Though this epic is silent,
it divulges the secret of Love, O God.

Please, open the hearts of nations
to receive the secret of my heart.

The Wind Became a Sweet Breeze
Sūrah an-Nūr (24)

I, the human being,
have set up my tents in the desert to populate it,
but a fierce wind attacked me.

It pulled my tents down, but I set them up again.
It blew my candles out, but I re-lit them.
It filled them up with earth, but I re-dug them.
It killed my children, but I begot others.

Once upon a day I came back from a hunting trip
to find the wind compassionately rocking my child's swing.
I was tired with the perfumes of sweat and effort.
I was pleased, and changed my stand towards the wind,
and my pleasure was followed by a luminous smile.

My smile kindled in the mouth of the wind,
and it became fire to warm and light for night.
And the place was lit by warmth and cold.

Trees blossomed and ideas were clarified.
We became friends living together faithfully and modestly,
forgetting our old hostility.
The wind became a sweet breeze in a luminous, open morning.

I took a deep breath, which made my breast glow,
and I disclosed the mystery of the fierce wind.

Protest

Sūrah al-Ḥajj (22)

I, the Human Being,
protest for and against my children.

The loyal among them develop themselves.
They aim toward honorable goals.
They silence the presumptuous; time and place are precious to them.

But the rabble of my children are selfish and repressive.
They argue with obvious persistence,
corrupting the hours. Indifferent to what is best in places and people
they distort life's honor.

And so I protest for the loyal and against the rabble
without denying that both are my kin.
But I distinguish between complementary pairs
such as vigilance and slumber,
and between incongruous opposites
such as cleanliness and filth.
I turned my interest from these problems of education,
and wandered through the forests of contemplation.

On the road of the seasons I saw monarchs and poets.
I saw a monarch mowing with the sickles of time.

I saw poets defining verbal projectiles and mirrors,
and lovers chanting them in pure happiness.

I was moving quickly into the depths of the forests,
the views chasing me even as I ran,

until I fell from a peak into the sea
and a fisherman rescued me and left me on an island.

I stood in silence, having come to my destination.
As if the heavens and earth were a pomegranate in my hand
and the light of Truth became a mouth
translating what I mean into all languages.

The Warehouses of Mercy

Sūrah al-Munāfiqūn (63)

I, the Human Being, confess to my love,

and open the warehouses of my God's mercy
and spend on those who are near to me on the Way.

I penetrate the pearls of the earth;
I erect scaffolds to connect the gravitations of space.

I open the stores of my God's mercy,
to build schools of truth,
and to purify history of lies and hypocrisy.

Hypocrisy is the tunnel of death in this life,
the disease of the mind known as schizophrenia.

The hostility between the overt and the covert,
a rape of the covert by the overt.

The virgin of the covert cried for help.
She is the one with chaste instinct
who could help the virgin's instinct.

The tempests of the universe are being calmed,
for the sun has opened her eye.

The helper emerged with a salvation sprayer in hand.
The old men, being aided, became healthy.

Children grew up; matters went easily.
The world recovered from hypocrisy.

I stood upon the lake of innocence
and responded to the overt light of the sun's eye.

I greeted all with the greeting of a lover
and occupied myself in the land of obedience,
and discovered the holy metals of the angelic realm[6].

---

6. Malakut

Your Comprehensiveness and Simplicity
Sūrah al-Mujādalah (58)

I, the Human Being,
have the profession of probing signs and showing evidence
to direct the hearts' spirits to You.

This is my evidence:
all that You instill in my heart and reveal in this eloquence,
and how You fill my life and being.

I turn my face to You and implore You
to substantiate me by means of You, Yourself.

My occupation is being alone
and purifying the places of solitude.
I chose solitude to be with You.

Day and night I open my heart only to You,
accompanied by the two tresses of Your virgin of sovereignty:
this world of witnessing and the hereafter,

and accompanied by the virgin of Malakut
with her free-flowing hair of knowledge.

In my solitude I glorify You by Your creative word,
and so I see the branch of everlastingness on the tree of eternity.

I have shelter in the shade of thousands of branches
in order to be steadfast and to collect the fruits.

In Your name I call for protection from all dangers
and seek refuge in all Your lines and letters.

Through Your beneficent bliss I speak
so that those who are addressed
will love You because of Your high inspiration.

I pursue the obvious, so I record Your signs in everything;
I foretell Your manifestation as You wish;
and I foretell the harvest of the tree of abundant blessings.

These are my occupations, through which my wind blows,
carrying sweet perfumes and intonations;
and by which I convince the creatures to be receptive.
I know the relativity of my knowledge and will.

Complete comprehensiveness and simplicity
are Your attributes alone.

I labor for knowledge and to inform others
that You are the Creator and the Bestower,
and that I am Your servant
who is liberated by being Your obedient servant.

I openly and loudly announce my feats from earth to heaven.
Please help Your servant as You will.

Satisfaction
Sūrah al-Ḥujurāt (49)

I, the human being, am not satisfied with anything.

I desire the orchards of currency, but they don't satisfy me;
I love the plantations of beauty, but they don't satisfy me;

I aspire to the knowledge of our ancestors and contemporaries,
but they don't satisfy me.

I'll be satisfied only if You are pleased with me,
if You set my mind at rest,
if You change my words by Your power of transformation
and adorn my hopes by Your power.

I'll be satisfied only if You are pleased with me.
Your gifts are abundant, and my languages are numerous.
I have innumerable praises for You.
I'll be satisfied only if You are pleased with me.
I restore Your land.
I flirt with Your cherished stars and orbs,
and help Your appointed prophets.

I'll be satisfied only if You are pleased with me.
Please be pleased with me.

And grant me whatever suits You.
You surely know what pleases me,
I, the human being.

On the Earth's Carpet

Sūrah at-Taḥrīm (66)

I, the human being,
carried the carpet of wind,
which took me to the pastures of Spirit.

I kneeled on the carpet of spring
and asked the Creator to make my pastures holy.
I've been repeating my kneeling and supplication
for thousands of ages.

Young plants grow in my pastures
and I enjoy their beaming brightness;

but suddenly, a mysterious death snatches them.
I cry and implore with a loud voice.

Between the tears and the call, new plants grow.

I've continued my kneeling and supplication
for thousands of ages,
asking the help of the Ever-Living, the Self-Subsisting Eternal.

I believed in His outward aspect seen in all phenomena;
and I believed in His infallible hidden aspect;

I believed in His First creation and in the Last,
and begged Him to protect my faith from doubt and unfaithfulness.

I thought of the journey of ages
while I was on the earth's carpet.
Carrying me through seasons
where fire is forbidden by the summer season,

but needed by the winter season,
and while I was continuing in supplication
upon this globe, I loved the heavens, I, the human being.

Creative Purity

Sūrah at-Taghābun (64)

I, the human being,
confess to my love.
I aim at that creative purity, which is moral sanctity.

The physical aspects are bridges and languages.
I heard of the sea that connects the physical with the moral.
I told my sons and daughters about that sea,
and since then, for million of years, they have been sailing.

The eloquent talked about what was beyond the bridge.

An economist spoke of fertility;
a sportsman spoke of power;
a politician spoke of leadership;
an historian spoke of civilization;
a theologian spoke of religion.

The essence of their news reflects the eternity
of the creative purity.

I polished the mirror of my soul,
and taught my descendants how to polish mirrors;
so they reduced the amount of dust
and treated each other with justice.
None of them wronged the other.
Windows are open for light and air to enter.
No dust, no fear, no need.

A military man told me that polishing had been achieved
and asked about the time of the march
and whether we had to march over the bridge or tunnel under water,

whether they had to take documents that determine
their affiliation with the University of Polishing.

I said nothing to the military leader,
for we no more need to march beyond the bridge,
since fertility has honored us
and its face has settled
in the polished chaste soul.

The Soil's Fertility

Sūrah aṣ-Ṣaff (61)

I, the human being,
arrange the generations in ranks,
and raise them upon this earthly globe.

I dream of the straightness of the ranks and their accurate alignment.
My dream has wings that soar and explore.

Moral purity is the objective of reality, order, dreams, and love.
I confess to the love of sanctity and consider my confession
the first line of an answer.

Who could perceive the holy meaning when sanctity is nearness?
The soil of earth is dense,
but it produces the seasons for the life of the living.
I raise my generations on the love of the soil.

I'm satisfied with the love of my children and their upbringing,
and the father of soil is satisfied with paying attention
to the qualities of his soil.

I invented the processes that regenerate the soil's fertility;
I cultivated with the machinery of truth and loyalty;
and I looked after it using the manners of truth, generosity, and purity.

I asked the Donor to grant me seasons of friendliness.
He gave me the means of dealing with others in religious languages.

I was astonished by the seasons and their yield,
and the winter storm blew.

I didn't know how to protect the seasons,

and so the hands of storms slapped me on the face,
and I forgot everything, even the soil that produces fertility.

In the heart of stormy oblivion Your splendor flashed.
You are the Lord who procreates.
You are the Guide to bliss and the Protector from harm.

I taste the remembrance of You after the storm.
I praise You for the new seasons.

I praise You because You are worthy of praise.
I declare my love to Your Holy Meaning.

Beyond All Images

Sūrah al-Jumuᶜah (62)

I, the human being, confess to my Love.
The sanctity of meaning draws out of me
the images of my confession.

I gathered my generations and made portraits of nations,
and brought them together on terms of love;

I unified meaning for them,
so succeeding generations have mastered the art of illustration.

I remind the congregation of their pictures
so as to arouse their enthusiasm.
I help them to surpass their pictures and their enthusiasm
and attain the love of purity.

A word is a picture of wondrous colors,
and the most sublime word is a word of response;

the most sublime response is the state of submission,
and the most sublime state of submission is perception.

The most sublime objects of perception are the qualities.
Easts and Wests come together in perception,
and doors open up between them.

I entered from the door of purity
and found rooms of praise.

Each room has a curtain,
and seeking forgiveness I attempt to enter.

Suddenly all the rooms were opened,
but none of those whom my soul was looking for were there.

And so I was saddened about the millions of years of research,
but after all my tears and desires had been exhausted,
my soul was cleansed with purity.
Light appeared and I was overwhelmed with pleasure.

I confess to my Love
and raise the visible above all descriptions.

The Book of Life on Earth

Sūrah al-Fatḥ (48)

I, the human being, am agitated by all the children's strange deeds.
I bring up my sons in brotherhood, but they quarrel.
I bring up my daughters on integrity, but they are deceitful.

Yet the ideals of brotherhood and integrity remain.
The truthful continue their struggle in my presence.

I am excited by the mystery of time,
and I look forward to the pleasures of discovery,
when I am given the ability to reconcile them,
when I convince others that fragrance relates to the earth.

Living on earth is a book,
and the mystery of time lies between the lines.
The stronger lines excite me.
Each has its own invisible power.

Hunger is a line in the book of time.
Sleep is another line, and death is a third line.
Who can overcome the power of these lines?

I look for the secret of defeat and victory.
I opened and closed the book.
Then I opened it with millions of resolutions in mind.
When the pleasant Face of the All-Powerful appeared,
I cleared the scales of my week,
so that You, the Creator of heaven and earth,
would honor my existence with the freedom of spring,
I, the human being.

At Your Table

Sūrah al-Māʿidah (5)

I, the human being,
relate to Your creativity and place my trust in our relationship,
for You are my lineage and my ascent.

You, the Creator who can't be imitated.
So grant me the gifts of the Creator's freedom.

Liberate me from the throngs of needs.
To You alone I entrust my throbbing heart and my thoughts.

I've arranged the table of thoughts
and gathered the appetites of all existent things.

I called You while I was anxious about my desires.

When You positively responded to my call,
You looked at me with compassion,
and I looked at You with total love.
So the table of thoughts vanished.
Perfect contentment appeared.
The banner of peace was raised.
And the earth will not sway
while the deep-rooted mountains keep it in balance,
and nourishing powers sustain the ascent.

Action is the way to unite richness with the heights.
I invite You to the table of my thoughts.

And You invited me to the table of Your creatures.
We were fasting when we responded to these mutual invitations.

You've created amazing innovations at Your tables,
and I presented the vast expanse of my table's appetites.

But my destination is You, O God, not Your creatures.
I realize You are watching me, Your servant,
and not the things I merely possess,
I, the human being.

The Fountain of Forgiveness

Sūrah at-Tawbah (9)

I, the human being,
see with the eyes on my face and in each second of time.
A prophet weeps over his son's death,
and his heart resorts to Him who snatched the soul, Allah.

Thus he is raised to the peak of wisdom,
where he lives in an ever-renewed joy, witnessing the mystery,
and perceives the goodness of human beings,
in the light of the continually forgiving Maker's management.

He fashions His creatures out of nothingness,
and desires pure innocence for humanity.
He places power within the human,
bestows wings of love and liberating strength.

But if these wings become toxic
with hatred and dishonesty,
the human slips into the swamps of sin,
where only repentance,
whose two wings are remorse and entreaty, can rescue him.

I turn to the Creator, the Fashioner,
to rescue me from my boredom and laziness.
I turn to the Most Merciful, the Continually-Forgiving,
to protect me from my weakness and arrogance.
Thereby He replenishes wells and opens doors in the sky for me.
He gives light to life, and so the fountain of life is lit
by enlightened water.
He engenders and cleans life,
by means of a maturing fire He purifies and enriches.

The fountain is the circulating flow of reward and requital.
I was innocent when the Fashioner had absolved me.
Why, then, did I slip into the mud of sins?
And yet I return clean by virtue of the water of repentance
and the fire of remorse.

I bathe in the face's eyes and in time's seconds.
I renew my arrival by my heart's prayers,
so as to see and surpass,
and be the human being that the Creator and Forgiver enjoys.

A Victory That Can Never Suffer Defeat
Sūrah an-Naṣr (110)

I, the human being,
collected the delicious fruits of the seasons
and enjoyed the pleasures of existence.

My conscience yielded fruits of ease and happiness,
and, with Your help, the varieties of my crops have multiplied.

I ask of You a victory that will never suffer defeat.
I opened the treasuries of life
and escaped from many tyrannies.
I prayed thousands of times in many lands,
and sat upon thrones of wit.

I dwelled in paradises of filial honor.
I obtained all that might come into mind:
lakes of perfume,
farms of hearts, and news from the unseen world.
These have been my activities.

But I stand with my nets on the shore
and ask the winds in various languages
about what is to be:
about success and triumph,
about a lake, about a micro sun,
about a truth for which and by which I might live.

I raise the nets and cast them into the sea.
The winds become still and rise again.
The waves rise and become calm.
And I, inspite of all the healing spas,
still await the medicine of self-realization.

It is that You may be pleased with me, O Life of my life,
I, the human being.

Swimming in the Waves of Time

I, the human being,
am attracted by the brightness of a distant morning.
In front of me waves of time are swelling upon each other.

I consulted my friends, and they advised me to prepare ships;
then they fell silent, and whispers arose among them.

How can we cross those waves of time to the morning?
Is it possible to swim that far? One friend agreed with another.

They dove into the waves of the ages,
swimming with naked bodies.

Using innumerable languages of love,
my voice became harsh amidst their chattering.

A coward, who hides within himself,
dreams of picking the fruit of love,
or a wealthy man purchases him,
or a passerby purchases him,
or both buy him with friendship and need,
or distract him with a portrait of his mother and father,
or he is called by the master of power to conquests and dreams.

And my voice became harsh amid their chattering.
I pushed away the chattering of the passersby,
and inhaled the warmth of freedom.

From deep within, darkness was breathed away,
and I inhaled the warmth of freedom.
From deep within, darkness was breathed away,
and the soul's flood did flow.

So the two seas were merged.
The two breaths became intimate,
and in the light of intimacy,
the brightness of Your shining Face came into view.

I glorified Your Supreme Name,
and glorification has become my way of swimming.
Soul has become the vessel.
I ask of You the Law of nearness and love,
I, the human being.

I Approach without Conditions

I, the human being,
approach Your creatures without conditions.
I touch the snake's poison,
and through my love it becomes a remedy.
I know that You are the healer,
beyond the two images.

I approach Your creatures without conditions.
I catch the fish of the sea,
and in the air, I change it into food.
I know that You are the feeder beyond the two images.

I approach Your creatures with no conditions.
I tame the wild horses of the sun,
and they become obedient steeds.
I know that You are the Divine Ordainments of Light,
beyond the images of heat and cold.

I approach Your creatures without conditions.
I unveiled the unseen so it became visible.
I talk to one person and another answers.
I understand from this that You are the director
beyond all intentions and directions.

I come near, or I don't.
I stipulate conditions, or I don't.
I laugh or weep. I wake up or sleep.
There is no escape but to You.

Noon appeared. The fires of Your creatures are increasing.
A gentle coolness belongs to You,
so please bestow the benefits of heat and cold upon us.

You are the Most-Kind and All-Knowing,
and I am the human being.

Imitation and Innovation

I am the human being.

O Gardener, is there really no other way to squeeze these fruits?
Millions of ages. We plant, harvest, press, and drink.

I imagine a contemporary world without poverty's borders.
Is this the perpetual imitation, or is it a true innovation?

Spring knows that it imitates what came before.
Why, then, doesn't it express some reluctance, or surprise us?
Autumn knows, and surrenders itself to the colors of its season.
Summer knows and happily gives all it has.
But winter melts its heart into tears.
These cycles give and take and repeat their prayers.

I think of a contemporary world without the prisons of death.
The sun has set, and so did the moon, and the father, and the friend.
Cups, pens, and ladders were broken,
and those who justify the loss
are considered innovative geniuses.

What is new in a familiar food even if you are hungry?
What is new in a mouth being kissed for millions of ages?

Fasting fought against a fig but was defeated,
and the shepherd handed over the lamb to the butcher.
The gardener handed over his virgin blossoms.
The young set the thrashing floors of their youth on fire.
The ages dance freely around the fire,
and the prayers are repeated by going on with eating and drinking.

I squeeze all kinds of fruit and eat many foods.
My breath is interdependent with the atmosphere.

I am sure of death, both in wakefulness and in sleep.
Has death ever cheated or deceived anyone?

I know that death has been true and honest over millions of ages.
Might it lie to us even once,
and make our age the age of fickle innovation?

The Worshipper and the Drunkard

I, the human being,
notice the Sun's entrance into her Occident,
like a bird entering its nest.

In my everyday I see after sunset both a drunkard and a worshipper.
The drunkard carouses; the worshipper, having fasted, enters prayer.
Each has a philosophy of his own.

Their discussions torture their father's hours,
and force him to spend on weapons to keep the peace.

The fasting worshipper said:
He, He alone has the Face.
The carousing drunkard said: I, I only empty my glass.
The worshipper said: I saw Him in both fires and darkness.
The carouser said: I'll wait until after this life to see Him.

The worshipper said: His greatness is my beloved,
whether in anger or pleasure.
The carouser said: My greatness is that I
must approve what He knows of me.
The worshipper said: I am happy when I meet him,
and so I pray to always be happy.

The drunkard said: I am sad when I am away from Him,
so I numb myself now even if my spirit will die.
The worshipper said: I live with Him aware of many veils.
The drunkard said: I make a home for Him in my blood and tears.

The worshipper said: I let Him suffice me.
The drunkard said:
I fortify myself with pleasures to be self-sufficient.

The worshipper said:
I see Him in sleep and wakefulness, above and below.
The drunkard said:
By drinking I outlive the dead,
so He's pleased to see me still alive.

I hear dialogs like these through thousands of ages,
but the father is never deceived by the sunset.
The colors of the sunrise and the sunset are the same.

To carouse and to pray are just ways of behaving.
Making the first ideal is to judge by race and religion.
Making the second ideal is a life of order and freedom.
The true judgment is made only by the wise,
but I am only a human being.

Threshing Grounds

I am the human being.

Our covenant is remembering.
Your forgiveness and blessing are threshing grounds.

The laborers at my farms bring their harvests.
The barley of charity is put on the threshing ground of Your favor.
The wheat of mischief is put on the threshing ground of Your forgiveness.

Whatever I plant is for You, because You are the Owner of everything.
But the power of my own motives drive me away from You.
I offer the fears that I have learned to Your knowledge and mercy.

Those who exploit Your resources confront me.
I protest against them, not against You.
And I make exhibitions of my objection in favor of Your cause.
They mention You at certain times,
but I mention You at all times.

At the time of wrongdoing Your name flows like a flood,
like a waterfall, like lightning, like thunder.

At the times of good deeds,
Your name flows like a stream,
like a smile, like a gentle breeze.
Remembering You is my balance and poise.

To be exact, I never remember You,
because I never forget You.
But I see You as Eternal,
and this is the mystery that suffices me.

I don't neglect remembering You at night.
And in the morning my only companion is Your name.

You do as You wish,
whether I call You or not.
I don't rely on my own memory or intelligence,
through millions of years, I've never served anyone but You.
Please pay the wages of this needy one,
Your servant, the human being.

Examples of Asad Ali's Poems
in the Original Arabic

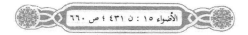

أَنَا الأَرضُ

شَهِدتُ مُجاهَداتِ الأَنبِياءِ في شُعوبِهِم

ما أَعتَى الإِنسانَ عَلى الإِصلاحِ

شَهَواتُ الإِنسانِ تُثنَوِّهُ جَوهَرَه

حاوَلَ نوحٌ طَويلاً في قَومِهِ، وقِصَّةُ نوحٍ وسَفينَتِهِ مَعروفَةٌ؛

ما سِرُّ العِصيانِ عَلى نوحٍ ؟

نَبِيٌّ يُعَلِّمُ شَعباً وهو مِن أُولي العَزمِ

وعاشَ قَريباً مِن الفِ عامٍ

ما سِرُّ الفَشَلِ التَعليمِيِّ ؟

أَصَوَ في طَبيعَةِ قَومِهِ أَم في طَريقَةِ تَعليمِهِ؟

يَقولُ : إِنَّهُ اتَّبَعَ مَعهُم سُبُلَ الإِعلانِ والجِهارِ

وتَقولُ القِصَّةُ : إِنَّ اللهَ لَبَّى دُعاءَه

فَنَتَجَ الدُعاءُ إِنْ فَشِلَتِ الدَعوَةُ

وكانَ الطوفانُ المُهلِكُ للكُفّارِ، أَتَرَى مِن بابِ الطوفانِ الحَربِ الأَهلِيَّةِ؟

ما عُذرُ الفِكرِ وأَهلُ الفِكرِ ؟

هل يَنفَعُ تَقويمُهُم ذَنبَ الطَلَبِ ؟

مَع ذَلِكَ يَبقى التَعليمُ والمُعَلِّمونَ ضَرورَةً

والقائِدُ المُلهَمُ يَبني سَفينَةً دائِماً

لِيُنقِذَ مَن يَستَحِقّونَ ورائِثةَ الأَرضِ؛

The Inspired One *Sūrah Nūḥ (71)* Page 128

وَلَّيْتُ بِطَلَّا مِنْ أَبْنائِي
بِكُلّْ قَلَتْ بِهِ مايَغَرْعَنِي؛ تَعْتَزُّ الأَرْضُ هذا الْقَوْلُ؛
بِكُلّْ جِدّْ دَرَعَ الْتَارِيخ
وَمَثَى كَالْحَقّْ وَحِيداً؛ لايَخْشَى إلاَّ اللهَ؛
يارِبّْ
الأُمُّ بِأَبْناءِ الْعِزَّةِ تَعْتَزُّ؛
وَالأَرْضُ كَما تَعْرِفُ دِنيا مِنْ أَيْنَ لَها الْعِزُّ؟
وَبَسِيطَةُ أَرْضِي الدنيا وَالْغَبْراءُ هِيَ؛
لكِنْ لُطْفَكَ يارِبّْ لَها
يَمْنَحُها ابْناً تَعْتَزُّ بِهِ

شَرَفٌ لِلدنيا هذا الْبَطَلُ
يُؤْمِنُ بِالْحَقّْ وَيُرْضِي الأَ مَلَا
وَيَسْتَقِي الطَّرفاتِ إلى الْواجِبِ وَالْمَسْؤُولِيةِ؛
وَيُسَيِّرُ صَحْراءَ الْحُرِّيَةِ
وَجِبالُ الْعَزِيمِ يُسَوِّي فِيها الْغَيْمَ بِحَيْراتِ؛
بَطَلٌ قَلَتْ بِهِ مايَغَرْعَنِي؛
شَرَفٌ لِلدنيا هذا الْبَطَلُ؛
الْعِلْمُ بِهِ يَحْضَرُ وَيَزْهُو الْعَقْلُ؛

يارِبّْ بِعِزَّةِ نُورِكْ تَمِّمْ هذا النُّورْ
وَاجْعَلْ قُوَّةَ قِبَلِكْ فِيهِ مَدَى الْمَعْمُورْ؛

The Hero to be Sung *Sūrah as-Sajdah (32)* Page 135

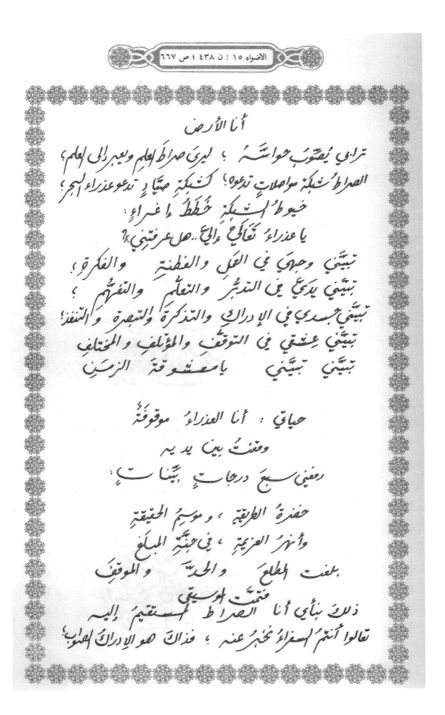

أنا الأرض

تراني يُصقِّبُ حواشَهُ ، ليرى صراطَ العلم ويعبر إلى العلم؛
الصراطُ شبكةُ مواصلاتٍ تدعو؟ كنشبكةِ صبايا تدعو عذراءَ السَّحر؛
خيوطُ السَّبكةِ خُطَطٌ ما غراءٌ:
يا عذراءُ تُغالي والجَّ .. هل عرفتِني؟

نبَّتيني وحبيَ في العقل والفطنةِ والفكرةِ؛
نبَّتيني يدعي في التدبُّرِ والتعلُّمِ والتفهُّمِ؛
نبَّتيني جسديَ في الإدراكِ والتذكرةِ والتبصرةِ والنفاذِ؛
نبَّتيني عشقي في التوقُّفِ والمؤلَّفِ والمختلفِ؛
نبَّتيني نبَّتيني يا مستوقفةَ الزمنِ

حياتي : أنا العذراءُ موقوفةٌ
ووقفتُ بين يديه
وعيني سبعَ درجاتٍ بيِّناتٍ؛

حضرةُ الطريقةِ ، وموسمُ الحقيقةِ
وأنهرُ العزيمةِ ، في جنَّةِ المبلَغ
بلغتُ المطلعَ والحدَّ والموقف
ذلك نبأي أنا الصراطُ المستقيمُ إليه
قالوا أنتم السفراءُ نُخبِرُ عنه ؛ فذاك هو الإدراكُ للقلوبِ؟

Virgin *Sūrah an-Nabāᶜ* (78) Page 140

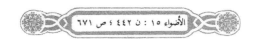

أنا الأرضُ

أراكَ في كلِّ قلبٍ تتقلّبُهُ

وبكَ أقصدُكَ   وأوجّهُ إليكَ

من قلبِ عصفورةٍ مبتلّةٍ ، رأيتُ رحمتَكَ المُدلّةَ ،

سَبحتْ بشوقٍ للحياةِ ؛ وبالماءِ لطّفتَ حرَّ نارها؛

رأيتُ ريشَها المذهبَ   بالشمسِ

تراقصهُ الريحُ والصمتُ   بالظلِّ

لأأتنعَ تحتَ السماءِ ملتقى الأرجاءِ

الشمسَ والهواءَ والنارَ والماءَ

وكتلةَ موسيقى تُوزّعُ الغناءَ

أصغيتُ للنبعِ يَبعثُ الأبحرَ والشعرَ؛

سمعتُ حنيناً يتقلّبُ في العطرِ؛

"كيفَ جمّعَ اللهُ   بيننا

بعدما كنا   بعيدَينِ ؟

أقدارهُ قدرةٌ حكيمةٌ حتّارةٌ ؛

لكنّها رحيمةٌ غفّارةٌ

تنهضُ بالبشرِ والذوقِ إلى فوقَ"

نهضتُ يا ربِّ لأطلبَ بكَ

لهذه العصفورةِ محمّدَ نعمتِكَ الدائمةِ ؛

A Sparrow *Sūrah al-Infiṭār (82)* Page 142

214

أنا الأرض

أحرفي مشتقةٌ من الرَّضى

وبالرَّضى أُشقِّقُ صدري لتنهض الرِّياض ؛

وفي الرِّياض بحتنـبـدُ العطـرُ واللحنُ والغذاءُ!

أيُّ جمالٍ أُفّادٍ يُغنِيَّ؟

شفاةُ الثمار العذارى

وخامات الأشجار اجتذابُ الرَّبيع ؛

وفي الرَّبيع أخبارُ الصدور؛ يَملأُ بي السـرور؛

كلَّما سافر بقارَّاتي الطامحون

كلما استنبتوا أنباتي وبناتي

أقيمُ لأسافرٍ ؛ بعزَّةٍ جبرونِك تُولَدُ الحروفُ مِنَ الحروف!

بذورُ الصنوبر تصيِّر غابةً

وابتساماتُ الناس تصيِّر أطفالاً

تستتَرُ بِك الأسـرار عن نظرِك

وبعفو نظرِك تستتَرُ الأسرارُ عن نفسِك

لذلك كنتَ القادرَ الستار

أُحبُّك ولن أبوحَ بالكيفيَّة

أستقيمُ لك كحرف الأليف وأوقَّعه لهويَّة؛

فثبتِني بِك ، بالقول الثابتِ والعمل الصَّالح ، يا قادرُ!

Birthing *Sūrah al-Inshiqāq (84)* Page 143